ALSO BY ELLEN MELOY

Raven's Exile: A Season on the Green River

The Last Cheater's Waltz

The Last
Cheater's Waltz

Beauty and Violence
in the Desert Southwest

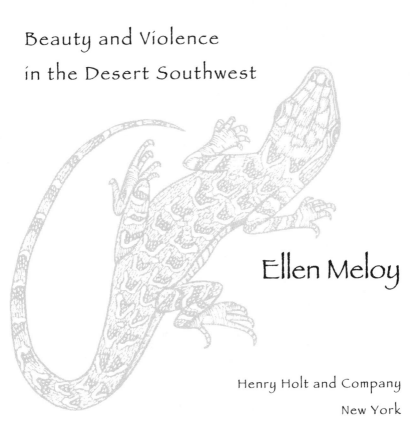

Ellen Meloy

Henry Holt and Company
New York

Henry Holt and Company, Inc.
Publishers since 1866
115 West 18th Street
New York, New York 10011

Henry Holt® is a registered trademark
of Henry Holt and Company, Inc.

Grateful acknowledgment is made to the following for
permission to reprint previously published material:

Excerpt from *The Theory & Practice of Rivers* by Jim Harrison.
Copyright © 1989 by Jim Harrison. Used by permission of Winn Books.

Lines by Masahide from *Cricket Songs*, Japanese haiku translated by Harry Behn.
Copyright © 1964 by Harry Behn, © Renewed 1992, Prescott Behn, Pamela Behn Adam,
and Peter Behn. Used by permission of Marian Reiner.

Library of Congress Cataloging-in-Publication Data
Meloy, Ellen Ditzler.
The last cheater's waltz : beauty and violence in the desert
Southwest / Ellen Meloy.—1st ed.
p.   cm.
ISBN 0-8050-4065-X (alk. paper)
1. Southwest, New — Description and travel.   2. Meloy, Ellen
Ditzler — Journeys — Southwest, New.   3. Nuclear weapons — Southwest,
New — Testing — History.   4. Southwest, New — Environmental conditions.
5. Natural history — Southwest, New.   I. Title.
F787.M45   1999   98-30325
917.904'33—dc21

Henry Holt books are available for special promotions
and premiums. For details contact: Director, Special Markets.

First Edition 1999

Designed by Michelle McMillian
Illustrations by Dorothy Reinhardt

Printed in the United States of America
All first editions are printed on acid-free paper. ∞

2   4   6   8   10   9   7   5   3   1

For Mark

Since my house burned down,
I now own a better view
of the rising moon.

Masahide

Contents

Prologue

One morning in a rough-hewn, single-room screenhouse, in a cottonwood grove but a few wingbeats beyond the San Juan River, I poured scalding water through a paper coffee filter into a mug that, unbeknownst to me, contained a lizard still dormant from the cool night. I boiled the lizard alive. As I removed the filter and leaned over the cup to take a sip, its body floated to the surface, ghostly and inflated in mahogany water, its belly the pale blue of heartbreak.

I sat on the front step of the screenhouse with sunrise burning crimson on the sandstone cliffs above the river and a boiled reptile in my cup. I knew then that matters of the mind had plunged to grave depths. I was either helplessly unmoored from my Self or hopelessly lost in the murk of Self. The problem, obviously, was that I could no longer make the distinction between the two.

It seemed as if I had lost all frames of reference. I had surrounded myself with a much-loved, familiar place, but lately it and I floated apart from one another, as if we shared a world in which gravity had vanished. I could no longer concentrate or hold life's focus or keep a coherent thought in my head. I felt desensitized in a body that had a local, if not a regional, reputation for sensory intensity. My social skills, always quite miserable, were becoming abysmal—symptomatic, perhaps, of someone who spends too much time alone, then deliberately plots to kill off the next person to cross her path with either a tsunami of mindless babble or profound, deathly silence.

Had I forgotten the point of consciousness? *Was* there a point to consciousness? Or could I be repressing a fury so terrible, it had rendered me catatonic? In Inuit custom an angry person expends his or her emotion by walking straight across the landscape. When all anger is spent, the stopping point is marked with an object, indicating the length or degree of the person's rage. What if my anger walk circumvented the globe, and I ended up tapping myself on the shoulder?

While I could not be certain if I was simply drowsily apathetic or enraged to the point of catatonia, I thought it best to cover both fronts by considering some kind of low-grade home lobotomy or one of those highly touted anger management seminars. I dismissed the latter, however, once I recalled that hundreds of stressed-out coconuts enrolled in such classes, dozens more overflowed the waiting lists—so many angry people on one tiny planet! Then I ruled out skinwalkers, satanic possession, indigestion, and a midlife crisis, thank the river gods, since in my personal cosmology the commonly prescribed antidote—golf—lay somewhere on a purgatorial rung below mall shopping.

The more I attempted to fathom this malaise, the farther adrift I

felt, an oxymoronic footless nomad caught in a slipstream of indifference that was so alien to my character, it finally scared me out of
my wits. Somehow, with a posthumous prod from a side-blotched
lizard parboiled in French roast, I had broken through the fog of
parapraxis, the loss of conscious intent. Objects are mislaid, the
tongue slips. On the way to find a paper clip, for instance, your
mind suddenly develops a block fault the size of Nevada and you
freeze midaction, quite baffled by the sheer impossibility of your
own existence.

No, my derailment was not neurological but aesthetic, a dulling
of the imagination in which even what lay closest—the land to
which I had so profound an attachment—had acquired the tones
of distance. As if by instinct I had long ago embraced the desert
with the full knowledge that neither passion nor beauty comes
without risk and that these conditions of being might well burn me
right up. Lately I felt less combustible.

I dipped my fingers into the coffee and fished around for the
solid object. To the side-blotched, fence, spiny, and whiptail
lizards so common around this place, I had become part of the
scenery, an oddly mobile cottonwood sapling or an unclimbable
post topped with hair and cynicism inclined to excess. Neither the
lizard nor I threatened one another, although on more than one
occasion I desperately needed the ability to skid across a ceiling
upside down. Whiptail lizards interested me because of their reptilian, who-needs-the-creeps version of immaculate conception.
Some whiptail species consist only of females, who reproduce
without males by parthenogenesis; their progeny develop from
unfertilized eggs. Side-blotched lizards, like the doomed young
one in my cup, are confirmed baskers. Warm stone, loose limbs,
daydreams, sun on your back—who can blame them?

I pulled the lizard out of the cup by its tail and held it up to drip-dry in the sun. I simply had to do something about this ever-creeping numbness of soul, I thought. I lived in one of the continent's extreme landscapes, daily embracing its aching blue space, searing heat, and voluptuous contours, all of which gave me the sense that somehow I was less encumbered than those who lived in greener, easier, temperate places. With its spare beauty the canyon country had always filled the empty spaces that test a person's heart with doubt. Here I could fit flesh to rock. The sole difference between me and the land was a membrane of skin.

From a box in the screenhouse I unearthed an artist's sketchbook with a hard cover and blank white pages and a digitally constructed, poster-sized, color relief map that showed every contour of my region, the Colorado Plateau, in light and shadow. I knew this 250,000-square-mile province well; sojourns and residence added up to nearly twenty years.

My home lay in its heart, the southeastern Utah portion of the Four Corners, where the borders of Utah, Colorado, New Mexico, and Arizona meet. It is a geography of infinite cycles, of stolid pulses of emergence and subsidence, which, in terms geologic and human, is the story of a desert itself. At one time the Colorado Plateau was as far below a prehistoric ocean as it is now above sea level: one mile, on the average. Aboriginal desert farmers who once held a fragile tenure on a land they considered to be the center of the universe changed their minds and abandoned it.

The region serves up the full paradox of emptiness. It has been considered a void, a "loathsome" province of little utility to humankind, and a kind of cosmic navel, an inexhaustible wellspring of mystery and spiritual transcendence. Epicures of fecund mists may starve here, but ascetics will not. Mesozoic rivers drown beneath rock and dune. Red sand and prickly history fill your boots, unbidden. The green in winter stays locked in juniper trees on the high mesas, and toads encode their flesh with silver, summer rain. The nights are coal-black and water-deep, the light often too bright to understand. In this abundant space and isolation, the energy lords extract their bounty of natural resources, and the curators of mass destruction once mined their egregious weapons and reckless acts. It is a land of absolutes, of passion and indifference, lush textures and inscrutable tensions. Here violence can push beauty to the edge of a razor blade.

My own slightly delirious life unfolded in the sensuous red-gold light of a magnificent land. The desert's humbling scale formed a proper vessel for chronic restlessness. "Encamped but not yet established" was how friends described me, although because I owned the eight acres around me, a settling trend appeared imminent. No, my world had not become too large. I had simply lost my motion within it.

I put the dried lizard into the pocket of my faded denim shirt and carried the notebook and map to a sandy bench above the screenhouse. Beside a thick stand of rabbitbrush I spread out the big map and anchored its corners with stones.

The map was lovely. Coppery reds, burnt golds, and tawny browns threaded with cobalt blue rivers and streams—precious few of them in this harsh, arid country. Pinched wrinkles of mesas, broken capillaries of canyons, great islands of snowcapped peaks floating in a sea of basins. In this map I saw my world with a soaring sense of its beauty, much as an astronaut must view Earth's whirling ball of blue below, so brilliant with light and life. The map offered a visual syntax of remembered journeys; it was my own movement in stasis. This, then, held a key to my somnambulism. Memory purifies experience, a map distills place, but neither memory nor map is blood. The silent chemistry of this desert lay deep within me. To reinhabit my own body I had to traverse, again and again, the desert's cruel and beautiful skin.

First I marked my present location with a small, shapely *O*. Next I reduced the Colorado Plateau to a manageable two hundred square miles or so around the home *O*. Then I outlined this perimeter on the map with a ring of fine red sand trickled from my fingers. A circle has no corners. So, to make my Map of the Known Universe portable, I transcribed all that fell inside the circle into sections and roughed them out on pages in the notebook, like an atlas.

As the sun rose higher, the cliffs shed their crimson light and turned flat and brassy. Tenderly, blue belly down so it would not sunburn, I placed the lizard on the map. The small corpse rested on our land—literally on the very dirt where my husband and I were soon to build our house—on the *O*, at the center of the circle.

It was time to get to know the neighborhood.

Tsé Valley I:
Alien Pebbles

A ny day, any time, I would without complaint travel seventy miles to see a claret cup cactus in bloom. The quest would not arise from botanical interest, from some sort of dead-butterfly impaling, snake pickling, tweedy naturalist curiosity. If you must know, I seek the claret cup—*Echinocereus triglochidiatus,* member of the hedgehog cactus family, also called strawberry cactus—for sadomasochistic pleasure.

The claret cup cactus grows in dense clusters of cylindrical green stems topped by scarlet blossoms so seductive, you want to but should not fall facedown into the lush halo of nectar inside each cup-shaped flower and wallow there. Each flower rests atop a nest of needle-sharp spines; each succulent stem wears a fiery sheath of them, deterrent to your lips and the tongues of herbivores. A mound of claret cups in full bloom throws its glory against the russet desert in brazen harlotry. Theirs is a wild and transient beauty of sweet, precise torture, an incarnation of the thin threshold between what the Zuni call the beautiful (*tso'ya*) and the dangerous (*attanni*). The flowers peak and wilt in a few days, and that was why I went traveling. On a seventy-mile loop from home and back, I aimed more or less for a broad ledge of sun-warmed slickrock that would likely bear enough of those gorgeous grenadine blossoms to drive me mad with love.

It gives me great pleasure to rise before dawn and set out on a remote, empty trail or road to a seductive place. A giant reef of tilted sandstone, the morning's lure to claret cups, ran north-south, jumped the San Juan River near the Utah border, then curved into Arizona like the tail of a snake. Its Navajo name, Tsé k'aan, means "upright rocks." Amid a confusing jumble of bluffs, buttes, and dry washes, it remained distinct for its resemblance to a rib or a spine that seemed to run around the world underground but just happened to surface here. I knew Tsé k'aan's midsection well; it lay a few miles downriver from home. The less familiar southern Tsé k'aan now guided my way: I planned to keep it on my right, cross it, then drive back up the other side. Except for the first stretch of road, which was paved, I would find my way on the unmarked maze of sandy tracks that typify Navajo Reservation backroads.

Slung over the southern horizon, the Carrizo Mountains floated above the sprawling desert, their flanks indigo, the last veneer of spring snow gleaming on their peaks like silver mirrors. I passed bleached white bones strewn along the roadside for several hundred feet, the boneyard of a sizable flock of sheep, although no one around here has ever been able to explain its history. Up ahead a hungry dun-colored dog, all head and rib cage, sniffed a roadkill but, lacking a spatula, gave up and trotted off.

Around me stretched the land of the humans—Diné, the People, as the Navajo call themselves—a rugged, elemental expanse of Colorado Plateau whose face is inextricable from the Navajo soul. The flavor of Navajo country is almost palpable. Human and physical terrain fit one another in an exquisite friction of conflict and harmony. What you see from the road is the land dwarfing the human: towering bare rock in bewildering shapes and vibrant colors and broad sweeps of rolling desert dotted here and there with a house, corrals, stock tanks, usually a hogan, and always a motley spill of junked cars, some upside down, some not, every car that anyone ever owned since the Korean War, lined up and sun fried.

I crossed a deep, tamarisk-lined canyon, a major tributary of the San Juan River and, rumor has it, the preferred route of skin-walkers on the move. These witches, also called Navajo wolves, are normal people by day—well, maybe they have an extra pickup truck or two—and evildoers by night. The Navajo feel great discomfort talking about witchcraft, not only because it is a serious matter but also because more than one Anglo missionary in the past prohibited the chants and cures that could protect a Navajo from such evil.

For vengeance, envy, or other reasons, a Diné skinwalker inflicts injury rather than a Faustian soul theft, often with spells or by injecting a foreign article—bone, quill, bead, stone, arrow—into the victim. Incantation levitates the projectile, which then shoots off magically through the air: a kind of Navajo smart bomb. In years past, the victim could be a car—not so farfetched when you consider the possible consequences of a disabled vehicle in remote, sparsely populated country. The upper reaches of the canyon I crossed have seen strife and tragedy in Navajo history, which may explain its concentration of skinwalkers. I understand little about such beliefs but admit that at night any number of inexplicables could careen around the canyon's sinuous bends on accelerated tendrils of an ill wind. I left the canyon behind.

Several miles beyond the canyon I turned off the pavement to a dirt road and started up a steep incline, slowing to maneuver the truck over bumpy, exposed rock slabs but maintaining momentum through drifts of fine red sand. The road climbed to a notch in the Tsé k'aan ridge. On the other side I descended a series of switchbacks, fishtailing and vibrating on a washboard surface so rough, my molars rattled and the door handles fell off. In places the curves were so tight, I collided with my own taillights. Partway down the dugway, I parked and peered over the road's edge to view the lay of the land.

Red sand dunes five hundred feet high piled up against the base of Tsé k'aan. Beyond them sprawled a valley that tilted gently northward toward the San Juan River, cut with dry washes and sprinkled with salt pans and sparse stands of greasewood, snakeweed, and fourwing saltbush. The valley filled over twenty square miles, with only two or three houses visible in the near distance. Close to the sand dunes rose a hogback with broken ledges on one flank—perfect habitat for the claret cup cactus. Several roads and faint tracks led off to . . . well, nowhere. However, it was clear that the public access passed close to the ledges. I would not have to walk far to visit the wildflowers, and I was grateful for this, not that I am lazy but because I was apprehensive about intruding.

An intricate, largely invisible system determines customary land rights among the Navajo. Occupancy and use, stories, family lineage, and small bundles of sacred soil bear as much authority as a courthouse deed; they recognize land tenure but not possession since, in the end, the land belongs to no one. Without the Anglo iconography of private property—survey pins, signs, barbed wire, gates, helicopter surveillance, remote sensory devices, half-starved Tibetan mastiffs—outsiders presume that Indian land is open range and that they can wander over any or all of it as they please. For this and other reasons some Navajo post areas, but for most the message is implicit: trespassing is rude behavior. I returned to the truck, bumped down Tsé k'aan to the quiet valley below, and stayed on the sandy, single-lane, main track.

In a poem from ancient Greece, heartstruck mortals describe their burning love as a powerful, transforming god that literally inhabits them. *Eros lives inside me,* one lover cries, *Eros's wingbeats shake my limbs.* One mistake in my reckless love affair with this desert was, perhaps, to invite a cactus to supply the wingbeats. Within inches of the claret cup's crimson blossoms lies a dense snare of needles. The hand that strokes the velvet will come away with thorns. And so, on a rock ledge with a delirious explosion of cactus flowers, my feast of bliss had to be visual and vicarious. *Tséde,* in Navajo, means "to be recumbent." I *tséde*'d across the warm sandstone and shut my eyes. I made myself into a very small bug, hovered over a bloodred cup, and, little bug heart pounding, dove in.

I dreamed I fell into a lobe of hell. Something horribly magnetic emanated from the rock. The flower's vivid colors struck like blows. To fend off my assailant I had to reach up and seize the blade in my hand, nearly severing my fingers to save my own life.

Wait! I shrieked, sitting bolt upright. I was merely seeking fundamental union with primordial nature. I was only pretending to be a bug. I was only trying to take a nap.

Around me all appeared normal—the truck parked nearby, a sandy valley nosing up to the foot of Tsé k'aan, slickrock ledges sprouting their gaudy wildflowers, including the claret cups, now filled with bees lurching about in drunken nectar stupors. A lizard scrambled up a nearby boulder, then turned to stare at me with the stoicism of a creature fully aware that *Homo sapiens* are oblivious to their imminent demise as a species. Two ravens circled above, and something—a toad?—plinked into a rain-filled pothole on the ledge below. Yet, like the religious statue, as inert and familiar as old furniture, that suddenly begins to bleed, or the cheap postcard photograph that pushes the desert reds a bit too far, my surroundings had changed. I had the distinct sensation of a suppressed vibration in the landscape. I would see it clearly only if I gazed more intently.

I picked up the notebook with the Map of the Known Universe and, sitting cross-legged on the sandstone, began to draw. Warm stone, loose limbs, sun on my shoulders, dreams—weird dreams— this was the basking lizard life. I waited for the peaceful radiance to come. It did not.

Red from iron oxides, the primary pigment maker in southwestern rock, dominated the earth's palette around me. I sat on the Triassic, a geologic period that is often called, for its ubiquitous and unmistakable sediments, the Red Bed Age for the Entire Earth. On an empty folio in the Map I sketched a cactus flower above rosette-shaped bursts of daggers, sheep bones, a toad, a toothy section of the Tsé k'aan anticline, and a rather fetchingly phallic sandstone spire to the west. As I inked in an outcrop in the middle distance, I noticed that several fans of rock debris formed an unnatural talus below a rough escarpment. The rim was dotted with dark holes—mine shafts and waste piles, I thought. I worked on the Map but felt restless and uneasy.

I set the notebook down and walked to the top of the hogback that held the claret cups. On its other side the valley stretched away into a hard blue glare. An intricate network of dry washes fanned out over the valley floor like dendritic veins, then fed into a larger, salt-lined artery. Cutting across the wash was an unlikely sight: the world's longest, curviest landing strip.

No, not a landing strip, a road. A carefully graded dirt road as elegantly broad as a Parisian boulevard, plunked down in the middle of wild, dust-bitten, single-track Navajoland.

I saw that my route, the smaller road, met the larger swath at a T intersection. I would have to turn right on the Parisian boulevard to exit the valley and go home. However, by the time I walked back to the truck and drove to the intersection, tiny invisible devils made me turn left. The fancy road veered southwest, aimed true and bold over the rolling desert. An uncharted route to Las Vegas? Yet the wider and fancier it became, the farther the road penetrated the isolated, desolate valley. Only one sign marked the way. DIP, it said, warning of a slump across an arroyo.

I cruised along this odd four-lane for several miles, passing a herd of pink sheep and goats, their fleece tinted by the dust and rosy light of their environment. A pickup truck approached from the opposite direction. The driver, an ancient Navajo man in a faded plaid cowboy shirt and Stetson, lunged down the strip, white-knuckling the steering wheel with the grip of a stuntman in a balloon-tired truck, four-wheeling over a row of Volvos. But for the spray of loose rocks from his rear tires as he passed, and the lack of about 15.3 million people in the vicinity, he could have been commuting to Los Angeles.

Although reservation dwellers want better roads, county and tribal governments have neither the energy nor the budgets to maintain far-flung miles of them. Thus, many routes to isolated dwellings remain slightly glorified goat tracks, dusty in summer, bogged in red gumbo in the winter. A wide, hard-packed, well-graded, red dirt freeway in the middle of the outback—I had no explanation for it or the next onslaught of topographical bedlam.

The big road ended abruptly at an enormous field of disturbed soil, put back together and recontoured with earth-moving machinery. On it could have parked all those jumbo jets that might someday take off and land on the ersatz airstrip. A smaller, more typically bad road, striped by the old Navajo fellow's tire tracks, led to a distant house. Next to the reclaimed field was an enclosure roughly the size of a tennis court but squarish, surrounded by a chain-link fence about twelve feet high. The fence undulated and sagged. The wind had blown so much loose sand out from under the steel corner posts, their exposed concrete footers practically stood in thin air; there was barely any ground left beneath them. It was a huge fence, it was not in good shape, and it was very strange.

I parked, walked over to the fence, and peered through it. Inside was a deep, sandy pit lined with wind-tattered black plastic, which at one time might have been laid down to prevent erosion and wind-borne dust. Tumbleweeds and a small pond filled the bottom of the pit. I could not tell if the water had pooled up from recent rain or seeped to the surface from a spring below. The pond shimmered in the bright sunlight—no skull and crossbones, dank salts, mutant plants, or dead bodies to indicate an alkaline or poisonous spring. Why such a cheap, half-baked fencing job? Anything and everything—sheep, children, Boeing 747s—could go in and out of the enclosure. The plastic liner was in shreds.

Then I thought of an even creepier question. This valley was one of the most parched places in the region—ephemeral rainwater in potholes, scant, widely scattered, one-drip-an-hour seeps, an average of about eight inches of precipitation a year, in a good year. Why fence off water in the desert?

The more I puzzled over this place, the more fretful I became. I paced about. Here I was surrounded by my beloved home wilds, yet here I felt unspecified dread. Dread, I supposed, can be part of the neighborhood, so I sketched it into the Map of the Known Universe. Then it struck me. Rock—it has to do with the rock. So a rock, too, flying about with a question mark, went down on the page under my name for this place: Tsé (rock) Valley. The garish postcard reds were coming back. I wanted nothing more than to lurch out of this aberrant, demented magenta blip in the desert pastorale. The lurch came in memory, however, not venue. From some dim, fuzz-clogged sector of my oversized hominid brain I dredged up motley remnants of knowledge and immediately lost most of them. At least one nugget remained in the sieve: Shinarump.

No one in the Southwest's red-rock desert can fail to be enthralled with time. Through the soles of your feet you feel an improbable, skinless earth cut through and through with the past, every rock so saturated, there appears to be no space for the here and now. The sandstone exposed in this valley went back 245 million years to the Jurassic and Triassic, periods that saw oysters, sponges, ferns, and dim-witted, three-ton lizards eating everything in sight and stepping on toothy, insignificant beasts still trying to figure out how to be mammals. Streams and rivers also flowed through these eras, carrying mineral-rich sediments in their broad, meandering braids and depositing them across the ancient plains.

Disturbed talus slopes below local mine shafts, like those I had noted earlier, often bear the distinct hues of a Triassic sediment known as the Chinle Formation. Set against the bloodred of adjacent strata, in a certain light, one variation of the Chinle's colors resembles the pale mint-green of Crest toothpaste. The Chinle Formation, and specifically its Shinarump member, is one of the most common uranium-bearing strata on the Colorado Plateau. I was well acquainted with the plateau's role, from the early fifties through the seventies, as a major producer of uranium for the cold war's nuclear arsenal. Relics of the uranium mining boom still lingered around the neighborhood. I lived in the continent's most bombed province, where for many years the U.S. Departments of Energy and Defense tested their wares on the western deserts.

I did not need my copy of *Nuclear Physics for Poets* to know that tons of raw uranium ore had been enriched into an atomic caviar that would, it was once believed, run my mother's kitchen appliances with power "too cheap to meter," keep a hot dog fresh for weeks, and save all of humankind from war forever and ever, the idea being that no one would ever use so unthinkable a weapon, even though they could and had and nearly did again, and had at one time kept approximately 43,900 of them worldwide to hedge their bets. I felt a tenuous gratitude for the remission of terror now that the cold war had thawed and test moratoriums had been enacted, and for the nascent attention given to coping with an alarming volume of toxic garbage.

The reclamation works and the red dirt freeway, possibly a trucking route, hinted at a recent cleanup. While one way to get decent roads is to be a Superfund site, this place seemed an unlikely Superfund site and a poor excuse for a Superfund fence. Whatever it might turn out to be, it was not likely to surprise me. I was, after all, a duck-and-covergirl born in the nuclear West. Nevertheless, I could not imagine that so serene a place could partake in so unquiet a century. In a strange convergence of human time with geologic time, pieces of this valley had been deliberately unearthed, piled high, and exported to fuel an apocalypse.

Instead of going home, I returned to the ledges, where the sun bore down hard on the slickrock and threatened to melt the claret cups into viscous pools of scarlet. They felt so reassuringly old, those ledges—petrified dunes burnished by wind and sand, cracked by heat and cold, sun and ice. When you are lost in

Africa's Kalahari Desert, the natives advise, do not try to figure out everything that is odd; scan and digest the familiar. I was not lost; I simply felt as if I had sleepwalked into an airplane propeller. How was a person to heal her numbed soul amid these fretful, querulous phantoms of mass death? Then I remembered the promise of the boiled lizard: to look closely and burn hotter, to forge the desert's sweetness and ferocity into my own, to find beauty.

The immediate task was to seek the beds of fossil rivers removed from their deep burial in eternity, to find the valley's missing pieces, now scattered far afield like alien pebbles.

I opened the Map of the Known Universe to a new page.

The Terrain of Strategic Death

Before dawn on July 16, 1945, a summer monsoon soaked a remote dry-lake basin, or playa, in southern New Mexico. Burrowed beneath the valley's normally bone-dry sands, a scattered colony of dormant spadefoot toads detected the moisture, unburied themselves, and in the darkness launched a scramble competition for mates, a search made successful by olfactory and celestial cues but mostly by the acoustic trigger of hundreds of toads, whose muscular vocal chords filled the desert with a concert of sound. *Scaphiopus* are explosive breeders: after rain forms ephemeral pools on the desert floor, they congregate in large, lovesick numbers for an intense period of reproductive activity that ends in oviposition, the release of eggs in free-standing water.

Thunderstorms rolled over the playa known as Jornada del Muerto, the Journey of Death. Puddles formed. The toads found the pools and one another. They straddled in a mating embrace known as pectoral amplexus and writ themselves into history in flagrante delicto.

Toward dawn the monsoon collapsed, as tropical storms will do when heat from a day-warmed landmass no longer feeds them. A few stars broke through the cloud cover. An eerie strain of a Tchaikovsky waltz from a distant commercial radio station crossed wavelengths with the only radio on the Jornada del Muerto, where on this day, at 5:29:45 A.M. Mountain War Time on the site known as Trinity, an elite tribe of scientists spawned the primary death anxiety of the rest of all time.

Trinity's progeny obviously was not tadpoles but a nuclear arsenal equal to a million Hiroshimas. Trinity is simultaneously a geography of nihilistic lunacy and passionate beauty. It is the locus of my century's strange confluence of deserts and physics, and I am standing on ground zero.

I arch my back and tilt my chin into the clear cerulean sky over this magnificent and awful piece of Chihuahuan Desert. I look like a parenthesis in a baseball cap. Directly above me are the ghost images of what was known as the Gadget and the underbelly of the sheet metal shack that held it atop the hundred-foot-high steel tower that was its one-night stand. The Gadget, a series of spheres within spheres, weighed five tons, including steel, explosives, uranium, gold foil, facial tissue, Scotch tape, and nearly the entire world's supply of plutonium, all of it pushed and joined, slipped and fastened into its metal skin by the hands of young men in their intellectual prime.

The Gadget was elevated to lessen the chance of its fireball sucking up too much dust, and it was stationary when it exploded. It did not drop. But it was a bomb, positioned in the same posture in which its twin, code name Fat Man, would ride over Nagasaki, Japan, less than a month later. Where I stand is where no one stood once the bomb had been hoisted into place and wired to its detonator cables, and the countdown had begun.

The Gadget's core—two hemispheres of plutonium joined in a single, grapefruit-sized globe—ticked away its half-life of 24,360 years. People, not nature, produce plutonium by reorganizing the atomic composition of uranium. Plutonium can be soft and plastic or as hard and brittle as glass, depending on conditions. It quickly crumbles when burned but slowly disintegrates at room temperature, undergoing five or more transitions on the way to its melting point. Inhaling or ingesting plutonium is a serious health matter. You can, however, hold metallic plutonium next to your heart without harm. Plutonium's steady alpha radiation produces a fertile, tactile energy. A lump of plutonium in your hand, it has been said, "feels warm, like a live rabbit."

Going backward from the atomic bomb in its tower to its rawest of sources, the plutonium core followed this route: to Trinity site from a converted icehouse in Los Alamos, New Mexico, secret headquarters of the Manhattan Project. To Los Alamos from the plutonium production works at Hanford, Washington, another Manhattan Project facility. To Hanford in the form of concentrated uranium oxide, or "yellow cake." The yellow cake came from raw uranium ore mined in Africa, Canada, and the Colorado Plateau.

I, too, have followed a reverse geography. In this particular foray I feel as if I have fallen entirely off the Map of the Known Universe, the Colorado Plateau, and landed in esoteric territory, this windswept expanse of Chihuahuan Desert several hundred miles away. By coming to Trinity first, I appear to be approaching home from the outside in.

A winter has passed since my visit to the claret cup ledges. Now I am in the Jornada del Muerto to chart the origins of Trinity's plutonium. By *chart* I mean not only the simple chronological lines of historical record but also a greater fullness of place. I have come in search of alien pebbles. I want to explore the desert that might have inherited them. Is my home inside the lethal heart of Trinity?

Three ravens cross my field of vision, erasing for a moment the images of the shot tower in my mind's eye. Strands of hair lash my cheeks in a wind from which there is no shelter. The broad alkali plain lacks vegetation with the height to slow the gusts, and there are few structures on this northern end of the White Sands Missile Range. This is wide-open Chihuahuan Desert, and this is also an enormous industrial complex of the keenest technical sophistication. In the San Andres Mountains along the military reserve's eastern periphery lives a rare and precious strain of bighorn sheep and, some claim, ecosystems more pristine than national parks.

The wind kicks up dust devils. Twenty miles across the basin from where I stand, military technicians explode something very frightening with a name mollified by a weighty burden of acronyms and loosely categorized as a "large blast thermal simulator." Except for two days a year, in a caravan tour under military escort, Trinity National Historic Landmark is closed to the public. The rest of this 3,200-square-mile military reserve and its airspace are restricted as well. On this February day, not a Trinity open-house day, the U.S. Army has opened the site to a poet and me. We are in the company of a Department of Defense public affairs officer and wildlife biologist, two gracious, unsentimental, delightful people in a business whose center is death.

Today on the Jornada del Muerto I will watch pronghorn antelope, falcons, and other icons of western wildlife, and later I will nearly be shish-kebabed by an out-of-place, spike-horned ungulate native to Africa's Kalahari. The stark beauty of the nearby Oscuras, serrated and dry and reminiscent of my home rock in Utah, fills me with pleasure, and the entire spiny chunk of desert gives me the creeps. This deranged jungle of ironies coinhabits my skull like feathers and fireworks. My heart fills with stones. I am the mad aunt who laughs her head off at the funeral. There rises in me the most inappropriate hysteria in this most somber of places.

It is said that history gave meaning to this desolate New Mexico basin, as if, until 1945, it was innocent of its own. The sterilization of landscape allows its reinvention; only at zero can there be a beginning, a blank slate to fill, even if the story that fills it—an apocalypse—itself becomes nothing again, in an instant. Land considered barren and empty of life cannot be stripped of life.

In my mind the terrain of strategic death will forever be desert. When I see a photograph of northeastern Kazakhstan, ground zero for the former Soviet Union, I smell the sands of the Mojave Desert and the saltgrass and shadscale of the Great Basin. The Cold Warriors attacked Nevada, New Mexico, and the Colorado Plateau, Australia's Maralinga, the African Sahara, China's Lop Nur west of the Gobi Desert, the Rajasthan in northwest India—regions whose isolation, aridity, stable weather, and exceptional visibility provided the geographic equivalent of "neutral" laboratory conditions for the largest physics experiments of the time. Common to these lands is a consensus of their worthlessness and the assumption that local populations were invisible, expendable, or relocatable. Paramount objectives throughout the era were weapons production and the utmost secrecy. A land dominated by silence and sky, dust and time, held those secrets well.

Jornada del Muerto. Not exactly a name to chum in the ecotourists. Manhattan Project–era New Mexicans read of it in their

Works Progress Administration guidebooks as a place where "few went" because "few wanted to." The basin's name came from sixteenth-century Spaniards who risked their colonizing hides for a shortcut. El Camino Real, their main north-south route between Santa Fe and El Paso, followed the Río Grande Valley. South of Socorro, New Mexico, the river veered westward and back in a long C curve. Travelers could save considerable miles by cutting off the curve, using a straighter, parallel route to the east through a parched basin in the cusp of the Sierra Caballo and Fra Cristobal, Oscura, and San Andres Mountains. Fierce heat, lack of water, and frequent skirmishes with the Apache could turn the detour into a blazing death march, hence, the Journey of Death, the Dead Man's Trail: Jornada del Muerto.

For every cold war kid, death-march topography sizzled in lurid Technicolor in the movie theaters of our childhoods. Gold-crazed conquistadors fried inside tin vests and helmets that looked like half-smashed colanders. A cavalry of sweaty but righteous blond gods chased pesky, unkempt people across an annoyingly leaky Mexican border. A grimy cowboy with a headdress of scrawny vultures lay facedown in fiery sands at the end of a trail of his own groveling claw marks, body flattened like a roadkill, his back a pincushion of Apache arrows. He rose and shook his head as if he had merely walked into a doorknob. Never mind John Wayne and his vultures and an "Oregon Trail" lined with the Mesozoic buttes of the Southwest, where the movies were filmed, or the Indians who were supposed to be northern plains Cheyenne but actually were Navajo extras in costume department Sioux war bonnets saying mischievous, naughty things in Navajo, a language neither filmmaker nor audience understood anyway, but which the interpreter onscreen translated as soberly as his forked tongue could manage, "We'll give you three cents an acre." Never mind the ecologically incorrect arctic loon cries on the soundtrack. *I loved that desert.* Hollywood served it up as scenery without explanation, but I found its palpable light and heat, its sheer geographic overstatement, far more familiar and intriguing than any hairy-chested morality play.

Off frame, in the West outside the theater and beyond the myth peddling, lay real deserts like the Jornada del Muerto, which real Spaniards crossed, and when they died there, dehydration or Apache were the likely causes. The Spaniards helped themselves to Apache homelands and to the natives themselves, as slave labor for mines and farms. The Apache fought back. When the Spaniards retaliated, the Apache harassed them with greater ferocity. The Americans took over the territory from Mexico, and they, too, dealt with the Apache in a brutal cycle of repression and revenge.

One of seven Apache bands in the Southwest, the Mescalero occupied the southeastern corner of New Mexico, including the Jornada del Muerto and lands along the Pecos River and Río Grande in Texas and Mexico. Aggressive and agile, the Mescalero were masterful tacticians in an unmerciful terrain. They were terrified of ghosts and the dead, and they tortured anyone guilty of incest. They launched warheads from strong, flexible bows. They took pride in speaking the truth, and they valued silence as a means to listen carefully. They seldom got lost. They were very adept at looting.

The Bedouin proverb "Raids are our agriculture" suited these mobile, elusive people. In language and behavior they made sharp distinctions between raids for goods and horses (a matter of property) and warfare (the taking of lives). The raiders paid ritualistic attention to avoiding the enemy by artful sneakiness and swift escape. Along with hunting and gathering, raiding comprised a cunning strategy for subsistence in a marginal land.

Barbed wire, the influx of white settlers with an army to protect them, and confinement to reservations changed the world of the nomadic Apache by the turn of the century. With the Apache out of their hair, southern New Mexico's cattle ranchers expanded into the central basins. A few trickled into the Jornada del Muerto and scattered their homesteads near artesian wells. Prospectors and miners, known locally as hill nutties, pecked at the rocks in adjacent peaks.

East of the Jornada lay the Tularosa Basin's rugged malpais, or lava beds, and acres and acres of gypsum sands the color of polished pearl. Like the other western deserts, these bleakest pieces of New Mexico's Chihuahuan Desert held little fortune for homesteaders who did not care much for starvation. Much of this land remained in the public domain, ripe for secrecy by virtue of its wildness. The federal government preserved the Tularosa's vast aeolian dune field at White Sands National Monument in 1933; critical habitat for desert bighorn sheep in the San Andres National Wildlife Refuge in 1941; and military habitat in 1942, as the Alamogordo Bombing and Gunnery Range. In the postwar years the U.S. Army expanded the reserve, now known as White Sands Missile Range, to its current two million acres, a chunk of New Mexico forty miles wide and a hundred miles long, over twice the area in Nevada set aside for nuclear testing. Sometimes called orphan lands, these vast tracts withdrawn from the public domain and sealed off for national security form an exclusive world with its own ethics and language and the restrictions of use afforded to private property.

The defense agencies that run the White Sands Missile Range today are neither desert ecologists nor aesthetes. They inherited the ethos that says arid lands are wastelands, not merely marginal but submarginal, places where nothing rusts quickly and the land seems but a parched void. Here few people can be harmed by hardware that is intended for maximum harm. Everything is out of sight, yet nothing is hidden. Both the spectacle and the secrecy can become intoxicating.

Latitude 33°40′31″, longitude 106°28′29″, New Mexico Map Number 44, Grazing Service, Albuquerque Drafting Office. Ground zero. I have had my first look at the Trinity monument, a plaque on an obelisk built from rough black lava hauled in from the malpais, and at the shed that protects a portion of the original bomb crater. I have seen two thick stubs of rebar and a twist of rusty wire that protrude from a small island of concrete, which is all that remains of one of the footings of the steel tower that held the bomb above the desert. The blast vaporized the tower and crushed its concrete pedestals several feet into the ground.

After the bombs fell on Japan, from 1945 until 1951, American officialdom suppressed evidence of their devastation and tragic human costs. It downplayed the dangers of domestic bomb testing as a nervous public began to grasp the implications of the new weapon. Radiation came only at the instant of detonation, the Army insisted, then "disappeared." To bolster credibility it showed the world that even the bomb's creators would tour an atomic ground zero without fear, though definitely not the ground zeroes with tens of thousands dead, dying, or ill. A month after Hiroshima, officials took the press and several VIPs into the once secret Trinity site. A publicity photograph from the tour shows remnants of a tower footing that are larger than today's two ground-level stubs. A gnarled cage of rebar rises from a cracked, barren, moonlike pavement. Beside it pose Manhattan Project directors J. Robert Oppenheimer and General Leslie Groves. Little white surgical booties protect their feet.

Plutonium, europium, cesium-137, strontium-90, and other fission products from the 1945 nuclear detonation, the world's first, lie beneath the soil. I carry traces of such elements in my own body, gathered in me and everyone else over age thirty during childhoods exposed to fallout from postwar atmospheric nuclear testing on four continents and the South Pacific.

In the midfifties strontium-90 from nuclear fallout began to show up in wheat, soil, and cow's milk. Humans also absorb strontium-90 into their bodies and, because of its chemical similarity to calcium, concentrate it in the bones, where cell damage can lead to cancer. Scientists referred to measures of strontium-90 euphemistically as "sunshine units." The breasts of nursing mothers, too, carried sunshine units. Bonded to milk, the most primary of life-giving substances, this formerly obscure radioactive isotope entered the household lexicon (every fifties kid could pronounce *strontium-90*), the public consciousness (protests against the health hazards of global fallout gathered momentum), and the pop culture (out of the petri dish of nuclear contaminants rose unhappy reptilian and insectoid mutations).

A decade of postbomb studies reported that the deep-rooted desert plants at Trinity and adjacent hot spots had absorbed insignificant amounts of the fission products, thus minimizing their spread into the rest of the ecosystem. In an environment with a high rate of evaporation and a paltry annual rainfall, the studies said, the long-lived nuclear debris remained minutely soluble and locked in fallout particles in the soil.

Immediately before and after Trinity, scientists were more concerned about wind-borne radiation than biotic uptake in vegetation they considered thorny, scraggly, and too sparse for worry. They hoped for low humidity and westerly winds aloft with a Bernoulli effect, or increased velocity, over the Oscuras. Such conditions would carry the radioactive debris from the blast away from the observation shelters.

In a world still naive about radiation's long-term effects, the team at Trinity worried about the short term. They prepared evacuation plans and posted military and civilian monitors throughout the Jornada del Muerto and outlying areas. When soldiers ran Geiger counters over a home in Bingham, they told a curious resident that they were checking for radioactivity. The resident insisted, "We don't have the radio on." Another monitor near Bingham evacuated his station when the cloud headed his way. He forgot his respirator. On the road he encountered a low stratum of dust. He closed his windows. He breathed through a slice of bread. To those worried about the fallout, General Groves advised: take a vacation.

Bunchgrass, tansy mustard, and Russian thistle in winter's olive-gray palette hold ground zero together today, and I am told that my radiation exposure is minimal. The Department of Energy, successor to the Atomic Energy Commission, produces a string of comparisons to reassure me that my exposure here, for one hour, stacks up like this: a smaller dose of radiation than I would receive on a jet flight from coast to coast; about the same amount as a charcoal-broiled steak; far less than if I smoked a pack of cigarettes a day for a year; several hundred times less than the whole-mouth X rays I recently begged my dentist not to give me.

My chances of developing liver cancer from eating ten tablespoons of peanut butter are nearly twice as great as the risk incurred during my visit to Trinity. Ground zero will expose me to less radiation than the amount I received from worldwide weapons-test fallout, which happens to equal my dose from sleeping with another person. (Body radioactivity, from food and water, is measurable.) Orgies and dense crowds can up the dosage.

In short, throw Trinity's half-milliroentgen (mrem) in with my 360-mrem average annual exposure from bricks, rocks, televisions, smoke detectors, cosmic rays from outer space, sadodentists, and my husband. We are expected to draw solace from the mundane, to say to ourselves, "Oh, Ground Zero. What a Regular Place." I cannot.

Ground zero in the nineties has at first an oddly pastoral luminosity—pastoral, that is, to desert denizens like me, who are accustomed to harmonious "emptiness" and therefore find nothing missing. Here can be felt a familiar geography of preternaturally bright sunlight, visible air, space capable of engulfing all reason in its seemingly irrational void: a terrain of the senses and of the spirit.

What I did not expect is the way in which this austere beauty concentrates Trinity's somber infamy. Dwarfed by this windy ellipse of scrub and sand and the vast open basin around it, the dark, obelisk-shaped cenotaph takes memory and rivets it to the landscape. My impulse is to lie down on the seam that joins the two, to drape myself over the desert as I so often do at home— *tséde,* recumbent on a piece of slickrock or a river sandbar, as a respite from the motion of a long walk, a way to fit muscle, bone, and flesh to a five-foot-nine curve of earth. The posture of intimacy and sensation evokes emotion, one hopes, which leads to meaning, then understanding. On this place of nativity, where meaning is needed so desperately, and physical contact carries a degree of risk, the separation anxiety becomes acute. Both of us— woman and land—are orphaned.

Immediately after the atomic blast, surveyors of the Trinity site described a depression that was 2,400 feet across and shaped like a saucer or the imprint of a cosmic sledgehammer. The 19-kiloton device, a mere fetus of a bomb in the coming line of more efficiently vicious bombs, pushed the earth down several feet. It obliterated every living thing within a mile of the tower. Its intense heat fused sand, gravel, and asphalt into a glassy solid the scientists called trinitite.

The soils of the Jornada del Muerto are predominantly alluvium washed down from the nearby San Andres and Organ Mountains, silt and clay deposits that date from the Tertiary and Quaternary periods. Trinitite is what you get when you suck up the Chihuahuan Desert and heat it to 100 million degrees Fahrenheit with a nuclear device. It is jade green. Silica produced by Joe 1, the former Soviet Union's Trinity, blown up in 1949 on the desolate highlands of the Kirghiz Steppe, created a sparkling plate of dark slag. Nuclear-fused Kirghiz is a blue-black.

In the early fifties the U.S. Army, never quite cured of a chronic indecision about trinitite, removed the trinitite and backfilled the Trinity depression with new soil. The Army buried the trinitite in garbage cans so the wind would not blow it to Texas. The first civilians allowed into the crater noted the three oblong hillocks that entombed the trinitite and broken instruments. In the sixties heavy equipment hauled off most of the trinitite to Somewhere, a place that official records cannot quite pinpoint, possibly Los Alamos or Hanford. Like the labs at Los Alamos and Oak Ridge, Tennessee, Hanford had been expanded for the postwar development of nuclear weapons.

The removal of seventy-three acres of atomic sherds to Somewhere reduced radiation levels at the site significantly. The desert began to reclaim itself. Grasses, creosote bushes, soaptree yuccas, songbirds, and other wildlife crept back into the hotter areas as early as two years after the blast. Although local ranchers wanted the gunnery range for grazing, the military retained much of the basin and continued to consume private holdings for its rapidly expanding rocket and missile programs.

Although visitors have pocketed souvenir trinitite for fifty years, small pieces remain on the site. Apparently the glossy ones are less radioactive than the dull ones. You will not get "radiation injuries" from trinitite unless you eat ten grams of it or hold a piece against your skin for eighty-three days straight. I am as likely to do this as I am to smoke 7,300 cigarettes this year or eat peanut butter or fly to New York or partake in orgies or visit my dentist ever again. One of my companions picks up and shows me a tiny sherd of trinitite. I do not touch it. I am thinking about sticking my feet under a high-pressure hose at the nearest car wash.

Gusts of wind Bernoulli across the monument and drive us out the gate and past faded signs with the yellow-and-black trefoil symbol for radiation. Behind us the ravens continue their nonchalant reconnaissance of atomic real estate. This time of year there are, of course, no signs of the Jornada del Muerto's toads, whose predecessors, fifty years earlier, performed the most cataclysmic coitus interruptus in amphibian history. Today's winter air and hard-packed earth surrender no hint of the sultry monsoons that lured the toads into the open desert, which they shared with, among others, the president of Harvard University, the inventor of the cyclotron, a spy for the Soviet Union, a number of brigadier generals, and a Hungarian emigré with the physics of the hydrogen bomb, to be a thousand times more powerful than Hiroshima, in his head.

Before the Army scraped away the trinitite, a broad platter of green glass distinguished ground zero from the rest of the empty playa. From a distance the glass gleamed and glittered in the sunlight like a pond. Today the desert scrub swallows the site into the horizon, and, as we drive away, I mark Trinity's general location against a distinct sweep of bajada, the brushy slope that skirts the Oscuras. We are off to another site related to the test. I wonder where the hell seventy-three acres of radioactive trinitite went. I wonder if I should mention beagles.

Except for a band along the Río Grande in southwestern Texas and fingerlike projections into Arizona and New Mexico, most of the Chihuahuan Desert lies in north-central Mexico. Ecologists include it as one of several types of North American deserts, distinguished by rainfall, altitude, and temperature. The Chihuahuan, along with the Sonoran and the Mojave, is a hot desert. For comparison, the Great Basin is a cold desert, spread in the continental rain shadow between California's Sierra Nevada and the Rockies. At the Great Basin's eastern flank lies rock tilted and stacked like saucers: the Colorado Plateau, a semiarid desert. For hyperarid deserts, try the Sahara or Mars.

Inhabitants of the Chihuahuan Desert base their lives on certain uncertainty. Their metabolic extremes—dormant slumber and brief, frenetic activity—closely match the climatic pulse of the desert itself, a biome with dry winters and more than half of its annual precipitation in summer monsoons. When the rains do come, nearly everything in the desert around you is probably having sex.

Chihuahuan plants propagate when moisture favors survival, and not necessarily in springtime. Among them you will find the prima donnas of the botanical world, wildflowers that reveal their showy blossoms only under perfect conditions. Desert flora generally carry drought insurance typical of xerophytes, plants that use very little water. They might spend long dry spells as seeds, then germinate when the wet comes. Many plants pollinate themselves rather than wait around for insects.

If you are a toad in the Chihuahuan Desert, nature has designed a simple strategy for reproducing yourself. It rains. You sing. You copulate. Very quickly. Water, the desert's most limited and unpredictable element, cues amphibian lust, and when it does, the toads must emerge from their burrows and find the precise location of potential mates normally scattered across the land like long-lost golf balls. For this they need robust voices. Indeed, when you reduce these squat creatures to quintessential toadness, you find vocal chords and skin.

The toads of the White Sands Missile Range fall into the genera *Scaphiopus*, the spadefoots, named for the digging flange on their hind feet, and *Bufo*, the true toads. Here live Woodhouse's, green, red-spotted, and Great Plains toads—all bufos—and plains, New Mexico, western, and Couch's spadefoots. They bear little resemblance to the slim-waisted, smooth-skinned, long-legged, and svelte, shiny, moist frog cousins that live among leaves or grasses near permanent water sources. Spadefoot and bufo bodies range in desert tones of brown, green, and gray. They look like chunky, warty, squishy dirigibles. You can (but should not) carry them around in your hands like a pork chop. When you think about licking them, change your mind. Some species secrete bufotoxins through their skin, chemicals powerful enough to cause discomfort, sneezing, illness, or hallucinations, all of which add up to an ingenious defense against any predator that wraps its jaws around what appears to be a plump lunch in a Baggie. Using its skin as a weapon, the toad might hunker down in eat-me position rather than leap away from danger.

Medieval folk remedies claimed that a barking dog fed a live toad would never bark again. Classical violinists in nineteenth-century Europe, it is said, handled a toad before a performance so that the toad's neurotoxins might paralyze the secretion glands in their hands and prevent sweaty palms. The Navajo describe toad physique and behavior in stories of an unruly animal spirit with swollen eyes, baggy chin, and rough body bumps he claims are hailstones and potatoes. When he smokes, the smoke comes out of holes all over his skin. When he attends ceremonies or social events, he brings his messy grandchildren, who swarm all over the place and wet the floor where people must sit.

Toads come wrapped in a complex skin that allows them to be aquatic and terrestrial in a single life. The aquatic phase is brief. As soon as a female releases her cloudy strings of fertilized eggs into a pool, her offspring begin an astounding race with evaporation. In short, from egg to tadpole to toad, the creatures must morph their little butts off before they dry up. Out here in ground zero country, an ephemeral rain puddle can grow a plains spadefoot (*Scaphiopus bombifrons!*) in thirteen to fifteen days.

As terrestrial adults, however, desert toads have all the time in the world. In sandy underground burrows they live on stored body fat, reduce their oxygen consumption, and elevate the osmolarity of their bodily fluids. A highly permeable skin stretched over smooth tummies and granular backs draws moisture from the soil.

As the soil dries, the toads compensate for water loss by storing diluted urine in their bladders. Periods of dormancy can last a week, a few months, or as long as two years.

During episodes of explosive breeding, a toad employs much of its body—robust musculature, sturdy lungs, well-tuned vocal cords and larynx, ample throat—as sound apparatus. The sound that arises from this stout drum of flesh jostles the air molecules around it, setting off waves of trembling that ultimately reach the ears of a potential mate, who will literally screw him for a song.

Toads in deserts and other open terrain have longer, more audible, lower-pitched calls than forest dwellers. Their voices carry across great distances of clear, dry air. Although individuals lie scattered about, breeding sites are localized; the rhythmic bursts of sound bring everyone to the right place. The roundup technique works more efficiently in an unpredictable environment than an active search, toad by toad.

Among animals that jump or fly or, like toads, live widely dispersed from one another, vocalization advertises the reasons for one's presence: territorial defense or seduction. Calls of distress differ acoustically from calls of advertisement. A whining, chirping toad warns of predators, and some toads and frogs "scream" when grasped in order to surprise their attacker into releasing them. Older toads have greater bass than squeaky teenage toads. A cold toad produces slower, lower-pitched calls than a warm one. Depending on species, toad voices can resemble sheeplike bleats, hoarse snores, creaky doors, squashed ducks, a berserk handsaw, or a pencil stroking the teeth of a comb.

Somehow amid the operatic din of a breeding chorus, a female hears the right song and meets the right guy. They then simply get right down to it and straddle one another like refueling bombers. If you must know, the male is on top. The breeding embrace, or amplexus, varies by species, size (females generally outsize the males), and the location of the orifice from which the eggs emerge to be fertilized. Doggie style describes the act adequately, with forelegs steadying the load. Using his nuptial pads—love thumbs with good grip—the male clasps his mate by her waist (inguinal amplexus) or more forward (axillary) or by the throat (cephalic) or chest (pectoral).

On the New Mexico desert in July of 1945, not only did rainstorms trigger a sex orgy among local toads, they delayed the test. Thunder rolled over the basin. Lightning lit up the shot tower, the inert pillar of steel that held the bomb, and threatened to short-circuit electrical instruments stitched to the desert with five hundred miles of wires. For the scientists who waited, the weather delay allowed time for nervous speculation on whether the bomb would ignite the entire atmosphere or merely incinerate New Mexico.

Then the weather broke and the countdown began. The Jornada del Muerto toad colony and a summer monsoon engaged in their ancient choreography. For thousands of years, since the early Oligocene, these amphibians had used seasonal moisture patterns routinely and successfully. Rain lay at the center of their biology; they had folded *storm* into their genetic code. Nothing around them caused disobedience to this amphibian wisdom, the imperative to unbury themselves from the sand to sing and mate.

Observers less preoccupied than the bomb makers might have felt themselves closer to heaven's air at the sound and texture of this rite of nature. Lying in their trenches, heads facing away from ground zero and eyes shaded against the coming bright flash, they filled their lungs with the aroma of wet creosote and their ears with sweet, unearthly notes from *The Nutcracker Suite*, which floated into the ether of ground zero when a distant radio station crossed wavelengths with the Trinity frequency. Yet so intent did they seem on the imminent mining of their long-awaited white light, the immediate world around them offered only counterpoint. The soundtrack for the ultimate evolutionary moment of this century, to which nothing on Earth would be immune, could not have been stranger: a Tchaikovsky waltz and small pockets of air pushed through hundreds of ballooning throats.

To protect oneself from images of the most extreme human misery, the mind hides on the wrong side of words. Over and over I read the same passage in *Hiroshima*, John Hersey's 1946 account of the effects of a nuclear bomb on its survivors. A month after the bomb leveled and charred more than four square miles of the city, Hersey writes, a lush blanket of green rose up through the wreckage. It grew in gutters and roofs and along the banks of Hiroshima's seven estuarial rivers. It rose up tree trunks and pushed into cracks of rubble. "Weeds already hid the ashes, and wild flowers were in bloom among the city's bones. The bomb had not only left the underground organs of plants intact; it had stimulated them. Everywhere were bluets and Spanish bayonets, goosefoot, morning glories and day lilies, the hairy-fruited bean, purslane and clotbur and sesame and panic grass and feverfew." Near the center of devastation, sickle senna grew in extraordinary regeneration, "as if a load of sickle-senna seed had been dropped along with the bomb."

By nature I am more apt to follow cords of pure sense than reason. I am more intrigued by a tactile universe, by the workings of a sand dune or a river or a torrid kiss, than the mathematical equation that packs nervous atoms into a warhead the size of a grocery bag. Yet as I move farther into the warriors' arena, clutching Hersey's panic grass and toads and other living bits of the

Chihuahuan Desert, I must adopt a vocabulary of abstraction, where matter is an elegance of numbers and symbols rather than things dark or light, spare or lush, as a child might intuit them. At Trinity I struggle to follow the Map of the Known Universe, to explore this landscape of consequence because I live in its heart.

Right-brained in a relentless wind, I sleepwalk through this two-million-acre, left-brained shooting arcade. A dense technical vernacular arranges the engineering at a neutralizing distance from the fact that much of what graduates from these testing grounds is designed to obliterate mammalian life, though no longer, one hopes, entire hemispheres of it in doomsday numbers. Military etymology is squeamishly devoid of human beings. The Department of Defense's *Dictionary of Military and Associated Terms*, which does not list the word *war*, defines "severe" damage from a nuclear weapon as "a situation that prevents use of equipment and installations permanently," which is about the same thing you can say about your new pickup when the fuel tank catches fire.

Although the bulk of current testing activity occurs in the Tularosa Basin south of here, on occasion sectors of the Jornada del Muerto will be closed to all but essential personnel. I doubt that officials have called off bladder drops or shut down noncooperative target recognition systems, kinetic energy penetrators, and "sympathetic detonations" for the sake of a poet and a congenital sensualist. Nevertheless, there is an absorbing calm here, as if it was Sunday or everyone was off bowling. February's pale sunlight further thins the quiet immensity of open desert with little but the distant mountains to hold it together.

Driving away from ground zero, we pass few human-made structures. This dry basin could be a howling wilderness but for a distant cluster of white domes and blocks near Stallion Gate, the range's north entry. One of the buildings houses a deep-space surveillance system that can resolve the washing instructions on a black silk chemisette 20,000 miles from Earth—or so someone once said. (For its analogy, the military prefers to use soccer balls.) Lacking either balls or women's entertainment underwear in geosynchronous orbit, the system tracks satellites and launch vehicle parts, lost cameras, stray astronaut gloves, and other space garbage.

Behind the numbing array of technology lies a fairly simple mission. White Sands Missile Range is a testing ground for NASA spaceware and for defense systems, many of which involve explosions. Missiles are fired and fired upon. Drone kits fly and land helicopters with no humans aboard, serving up airborne targets. If the drone helicopters wander off disobediently toward Las Cruces or El Paso, they will self-destruct. Experimenters simulate atomic blasts with massive explosions of ammonium nitrate (fertilizer) and fuel oil, or ANFOs, and a thermal hell of 5,000 degrees Fahrenheit, energized by a solar furnace. Nearly every weapon and vehicle in the U.S. arsenal, down to its rivets and paint job, has been subjected to a nuclear environment without actually popping another real one on the Jornada del Muerto.

Self-propelled warheads made up of a thousand "bomblets," smart munitions, Patriot missiles, Stealth bombers, and other new breeds of "tactically agile" hardware run through their paces on White Sands, one of the largest overland testing ranges in the United States. A gluey quagmire of acronyms induces brain death long before I reach their full names or hear how they work or what they do. This is a brilliant security technique, I believe, since few of us would remain conscious past jargon fortresses such as GBFEL-TIE, FAADS, AMRAMMS, and ATACMS or look up from our televisions if someone burst into the room and yelled "Blast overpressure!" (nuclear attack).

Nearly every missile and rocket in the cold war arsenal came of age here—Viking, Hermes, Nike, and others. Experiments known as the Albert flights strapped four monkeys and a mouse into rocket payloads and blasted them skyward. The primates, including the rhesus monkey Albert, for whom the series was named, experienced no ill effects from rocket travel unless you count certain phases of the experiment: three of the monkeynauts survived their flights only to die on impact when their parachutes failed.

Although my rational mind understands that such tests significantly narrowed the risks for humans, they seldom fail to arouse in me certain animal anxieties. Burning in a memory from childhood, for instance, is a photograph of a long row of rabbits confined from the neck down in a large white metal boxes. An officious-looking technician in a lab coat, carrying a clipboard and a hypodermic needle as long as an angler's fly rod, walked the row. The purpose of the experiment has been lost to memory. At the time, however, I thought the rabbits were trapped in washing machines, their small bodies pummeled senseless by the spin cycle, their pitiful cries stifled by drugs. Beyond pummeled bunnies stalked more images of torment: millions of rats martyred to doctoral dissertations and FDA ratings; chickens strapped to little Frankenstein tables, their beaks smeared with lipstick to test the toxicity of cosmetics; chimpanzees forced to smoke ten packs of Marlboros a day or to stand haunch-deep in industrial cleaning products.

In the years after Hiroshima and Nagasaki, other human beings were involved in radiation experiments, among them 220,000 soldiers who witnessed bomb tests and eighteen hospital patients who were given small doses of plutonium without their informed consent in a government experiment undertaken from 1945 to 1947. However, at research facilities in Albuquerque, north of

Trinity, and at various western universities, the beagle was the test species of choice. To determine how mammals metabolized radioactive contaminants, lab beagles consumed atomic snacks by injection, ingestion, or inhalation. The same attribute that gives the beagle its stamina as a hunter—a large lung-to-body ratio—made it desirable for biomedical research. It also provided a model more germane to humans than rats. It lived long enough to develop tumors for study. Like humans, it excreted the plutonium that did not stick to its lungs or migrate to its skeleton. Beagle studies once and for all established plutonium's deadly bone-seeking properties and generated data that helped set exposure limits for workers in the nuclear industries.

The beagle is a lowbrow, stubborn, all-purpose hunting dog, not as effete as a bird dog and much less likely to drool on you from the backseat of a car. Out here on the Jornada del Muerto, a beagle seems as likely as a pod of octopi in retro-Hawaiian surf trunks. Yet this little dog was no lipstick tester. As a topic, lab animal disposal has a way of killing polite conversation, so, in the end, conscious of my lowly status as a scalder of lizards, I do not ask my hosts about this member of the nuclear bestiary. I am not sure I want to know the precise fate of over four decades of cold war beagles. The beagles and their radioactive poop have joined the nuclear waste stream—gloves, booties, pipe wrenches, soil, fuel rods, warheads—squirreled away to Somewhere or ever in search of a sepulcher.

Since my companions and I are still within the boundaries of the Trinity National Historic Landmark, the bare patches of desert I see from the road are more likely to be salt pans than beagle dumps or WITs (Warhead Impact Targets) or bombing ranges known by names such as Sting, Queen 15, Yonder, Red Rio, and White Sands National Monument. The broad expanse of desert appears frail against the vast amount of trial and precaution needed to accommodate the machinery of aggression. Americans have devoted more acreage of public domain to military reserves than to all national parks combined. The heart of modern warfare has resided in these large tracts of de facto wilderness for over half a century. Since we are not allowed into this land, we cannot know it intimately. Yet to westerners it is familiar terrain, a neighborhood, so to speak, of aggressive fears and unimaginable weapons parked in the "empty" space that is our glory. Familiarity tempers the friction between war laboratory and landscape, terror and the sublime, into an oddly harmonious anarchy. I am visiting nuclear ground zero, *and* I am touring a rather pleasant zoo.

This incongruous geography—shrapnel in the greasewood, antelope in the WITs, toads above the plutonium—seldom raises hairs of irony among its caretakers. If you give the sun's copper glare your best Clint Eastwood squint (ignoring, for a moment, the local nuclear environment simulator, the toxic muck routinely involved in weapons testing, here and there a chromium or diesel spill, and the fact that many defense activities remain exempt from oversight by environmental regulatory agencies), you will find on this tract of desert a distinctly western blend of environmental chauvinism and fatal carelessness.

After thirty years of weapons frenzy following World War II, environmental laws in the seventies began to impose controls on public lands under military jurisdiction. A team of biologists now protects the range's sensitive habitats from the bombs, guns, missiles, and cannons fired by their colleagues. The biologists, among them Daisan Taylor, one of my hosts on the Trinity tour, track wild creatures as they breed, nest, and feed. They monitor the big-game hunts allowed on portions of the missile range each year.

Tests that might disturb antelope as they rut or drop their kids are relocated or rescheduled on a biologist's recommendation. The Army fences off heavy-use impact areas from animals and in some instances scares them away with loud noises lest they be imperiled by missile strikes or ANFO'd heavenward in surprise and pain. Park rangers from the White Sands National Monument fly aerial reconnaissance with Army pilots, seeking old warheads or crashed jet drones and the missiles that shot them down. Recovery teams then move in to clean up the pieces.

A staff archaeologist, who has undertaken a rangewide survey of sites that encompass nine thousand years of human occupation, protects cultural remnants of Pueblo, Apache, Hispanic, Anglo, and other peoples against devices designed to microwave aggressive, adversarial postmodern peoples with high-energy lasers. Restricted public access, the 259th Military Police Company, and sophisticated surveillance systems against enemy infiltration free him from worry about pot hunters and vandals.

Excluding areas of direct and messy hits, the Army's fifty-year protective seal has kept a considerable chunk of Chihuahuan Desert in a remarkably wild state. Before the gunnery range was created in the early forties, heavy livestock use diminished semi-arid grasslands and encouraged the invasion of creosote, mesquite, and exotics such as tumbleweed and cheatgrass, all of which can alter the dynamic equilibrium of a native plant community. However, on several thousand square miles of New Mexico, bovine ecologists have been absent for five decades—an eon by rangeland standards, though possibly not enough time to determine if the disruption of native flora has exceeded their ability to regenerate. In other words, the mesquite and creosote have not left yet.

Plants in remote sectors of the missile range grow amid sonic booms and munching native herbivores. The San Andres Mountains, where few humans may tramp about, contain the entire habitat of a cactus called Sandberg's pincushion. On the bajadas of the Oscura Mountains above the Trinity site, grasslands rich with native black grama flourish. Nearby lies a nine-by-six-mile bombing range. By some bizarre logic, one of the world's biggest arms dealers now holds in reserve an indigenous desert herbarium.

In this vehicle moving away from ground zero, I traverse an ocean of sediment zippered with irregular block faults, some of them uplifted in isolated, north-south-running mountain ranges, and underlined by an east-west expansion, a stretching apart too slow to feel, of course, but geologically tense—in short, classic basin and range geography. Where the province extends its southernmost crimp-and-swath rhythm into New Mexico, the White Sands Missile Range includes a fair share of it: two basins (the Jornada and the Tularosa) and several mountain ranges. The predominant range, the San Andres Mountains, forms an asymmetrical rib of rock eighty-five miles long, a relatively undisturbed montane ecosystem within the military reserve.

Cenozoic alluvium and debris sloughed off from the surrounding mountains or washed in by the Río Grande before the river shifted west to its present channel a million years ago fill the hot, flat heart of the Jornada. The Tularosa's dry lake bed gleams with gypsum sands. The middle worlds between alkali flats and high peaks support grassland, malpais, sand dune, bajada, canyon, and other habitats.

On these lands roam mule deer, bobcats, and one of the healthiest cougar populations in the West. Golden eagles, kit foxes, gray foxes, coyotes, and feral horses. Prairie rattlers and diamondbacks. Click beetles and fire ants. Panic grass and Mescalero milkwort.

Peyote, cholla, and a stocky, barrel-shaped cactus known as a horse crippler. A carnivorous little mouse that stands on its hind legs, throws its head back, flattens its tiny ears against its head, and howls. Assorted bats, bunnies, bufos, and reptiles. On my day at Trinity I am cruising through the only place on Earth where a rare race of North American sheep shares a wilderness with two particle accelerators.

The sun is high now, suffusing the Oscuras' erosion-carved face with a bright, flat light. We leave ground zero in our wake and enter an all-American, generic desert experience: nature from the tarmac at just under sixty miles an hour. This is the velocity of glimpses—a black-tailed jackrabbit sprinting between clumps of saltbush, a dust devil bearing leaf bits in its whirling wraith, ragged peaks on one horizon, a curving rim of earth on the other, rippling in the light of a weak winter mirage. Suddenly the roadside explodes with the white rumps of a dozen pronghorn antelope. By flexing certain skin muscles, antelope can hold their pelages at different angles. In unison they stand their flashy butt hairs on end, flicking a danger signal far across the flats. Instantly the animals lope at an easy forty miles per hour (they are capable of seventy), spooked by our vehicle and a passing snow-white, eighteen-wheel semitrailer that bristles with a thicket of rods, satellite dishes, cables, and antennae so dense, I swear I can hear a crackling, eavesdropping static from the day's traffic in extra-terrestrial lingerie. The antelope slow their pace and eventually resume their browse at a safer distance.

At the center of antelope biology lies open space. Bodies de-signed for full-on forward locomotion simply do not work with trees or walls. Antelope rarely interrupt this fluid trajectory to pogo over a barbed wire fence. Instead, they usually belly-slide under the bottom strand, on the run. Exceptional eyesight alerts them to danger in broad, brushy basins like the Jornada del Muerto. Antelope eyes are pools of deep, inscrutable velvet. Long, thick lashes protect them from dust. The dark orbs cool their brains in desert heat. Set away from the face by protruding bones, these eyes bring the antelope its world: the geography of long distances. Here the terrain of strategic death tenders distance in abundance.

A few miles beyond the first herd we stop to observe a second group, a buck and his harem, engaged in watchful feeding. They turn their handsome heads and stare at us curiously. Curiosity, in fact, might be a grossly underestimated antelope trait. If you are not carrying a gun and you do something mildly nonsensical within their view—maybe lie on your back in the sagebrush and kick around your arms and legs like an overturned turtle—an ante-lope might just trot right up to you, wondering what the hell you are doing.

Before I can leap out of the car and try this, one of my guides, Army public affairs director Jim Eckles, diverts my attention to a T-shaped wooden post beside the road, one of the few remaining posts of Trinity vintage. Barely six feet tall and weathered to the silver of an old juniper fence, the T post that once carried a taut skein of wires to the shot tower now holds a perched raptor.

We identify the bird as a kestrel, a small western falcon. Its larger cousin, the peregrine falcon, lived in the nearby San Andres Mountains until the late sixties, when the world's peregrine population crashed due to adverse reactions to pesticides. Recent surveys on the missile range have identified potential peregrine habitat but no aeries. Peregrine falcons prefer cliffs. The bird more likely to fill the Jornada del Muerto's resident falcon niche is the northern aplomado, a subspecies of aplomado falcon, a grassland raptor that frequents savannas and desert scrub, and nests in stick platforms in small trees. Aplomado falcons once ranged from the southern reaches of U.S. border states to Chile. These days they are so scarce that endangered species laws protect them.

Thus far none of the local species in the hierarchy of official protection—no Oscura Mountain land snail or New Mexico meadow jumping mouse, no rock daisy or Los Olmos tiger beetle—has brought the Army to its knees. Should a pair of aplomado falcons fly into the White Sands grid and settle into a stick nest, however, the generals would have to pay attention.

The problem with the missile range bestiary is that you cannot simply trek across the creosote flats until your feet are bloody pulps, earning glimpses of an elusive bovid or scrabbling reptile. Here a wildlife tour assumes scrapbook form, a collection of images garnered from documents and biologists with security clearances. Until the Army is no longer landlord of this unlikely wildlife preserve, the naturalist must be satisfied with imagination.

Along with the aplomado falcon, another protected species, piscine and about the size of a paper clip, spices up the generals' fauna. This one is easier to protect (and, for the same reasons, to annihilate) because it does not fly around a country or two and because it has never left what has been the entire extent of its range for the past several thousand years. The White Sands pupfish *(Cyprinodon tularosa)* lives in a few isolated, spring-fed pools and creeks in the Tularosa Basin, relic waters of the Pleistocene lake that once covered the basin's interior. Calcium-tolerant kidneys and an extraordinary thermoregulatory system packed into its tiny frame adapt the pupfish to hot, salty habitat. A toxic spill, predation by exotics, or dewatering the pools could destroy the world's population of this species. Since 1945, one atomic bomb and more than fifty thousand missile firings have missed.

Like an island of mountains inside an ocean of human incursions, the San Andres lie mostly within the White Sands Missile Range. In their southern reaches the spacious San Andres National Wildlife Refuge once preserved all that remained of native Mexican bighorn sheep in the Chihuahuan Desert this side of the Mexican border. Perhaps you are thinking of a few hundred remnant animals, not all in one place at once but in scattered bands, elusive and comfortable in their spacious, lofty highlands of cliffs and broad vistas, for desert bighorns favor places with unobstructed views. If you imagine a few hundred sheep, you will be wrong. Imagine the twenty to thirty animals of 1991—you will still be wrong. Imagining the San Andres "herd" is, in fact, unimaginable because it is quite possible that only one sheep remains. *One.*

Although restricted public access and the corral of land around the bighorns protected them, this isolation, a genetic as well as a physical one, also weakened them. Their enclave stranded them from the infrequent but necessary outmigrations that take advantage of new habitat and genetic intermixing, according to wildlife biologist Paul Krausman. The herd on its island became susceptible to predators, parasites, and disease. In 1993, as bighorn numbers dwindled, Krausman wrote, "The [San Andres] herds cannot be naturally replenished from adjacent ranges, so there is no relief valve for the sheep on the mountain. They are not headed for the last roundup; they are in it."

The terms *desert bighorn* and *mountain bighorn* distinguish the sheep that live in the arid highlands of the Southwest and Mexico from the larger, more abundant Rocky Mountain bighorn sheep in the intermountain West and northern Rockies. Biologists group four races, or subspecies, under the common name desert bighorn.

By virtue of a mutual dependence on similar topography—dry, unpopulated land—many of the Southwest's desert bighorns share territory with the U.S. Department of Defense, on refuges within or adjacent to bombing ranges in Arizona, Nevada, and New Mexico. Perhaps no other large mammal is the subject of field studies punctuated by artillery fire, sonic booms, the strafing of jets, or the scream of rockets. To these disturbances the bighorns are either oblivious or susceptible, depending on whom you ask and whom they work for. One school of thought claims that the war games hardly arouse a sheep hair. Others believe that the military racket stresses the sheep so severely, they fail to eat or reproduce or they lose their footing and fall off cliffs.

The San Andres desert bighorns *(Ovis canadensis mexicana)* were remnants of populations that once ranged the rugged mountains in southern New Mexico and in Chihuahua and Coahuila in old Mexico. Rapidly shrinking habitat and herds prompted hunting restrictions and the establishment of the San Andres National Wildlife Refuge in 1941. Sheep numbers rose in the fifties, then crashed. A similar population spike and crash occurred in the seventies. Biologists relate both events to severe outbreaks of scabies.

Scabies infestations may have been cyclical among desert bighorns before human influence, but little is known about the relationship between the scabies mite parasite and its host or how an infestation begins. (Domestic livestock and proximity to mule deer might be factors.) Historically, even high mortality from scabies left enough sheep to sustain the population. During past die-offs, refuge managers pulled some of the sheep off the range, treated them, then released them back into the mountains. The latest infestation of scabies, exacerbated by drought and heavy predation, pushed the remnant herd across a threshold into numbers and vigor so low, it could not recover.

San Andres Ewe 067, identified by the frequency on her radio collar, is nine years old. As a three-year-old, when she was captured and fit with the collar that verifies her existence, she broke her leg. But she healed; she is a survivor. She carries the last of the San Andres' *Ovis canadensis mexicana* gene pool in situ, in the wild, in her native range. Wildlife officials prefer to believe that the rugged mountains hide her companions—bighorn sheep are elusive and difficult to find—yet during more than two years of ground and helicopter surveys, and on film taken by cameras posted at known water holes, no other desert bighorns have been seen. Krausman's last roundup is this solitary ewe. She will be caught, vaccinated, and quarantined. The refuge established specifically to protect her race will have no desert bighorns until transplants from other parts of New Mexico restock the range.

The top carnivore on the White Sands food chain has been altogether absent since the forties. Decades of predator control eradicated the Mexican gray wolf *(Canis lupus baileyi)* from its historic American range, leaving a remnant population in Mexico. Recovery programs now seek to bring these wolves back to habitat deemed biologically and politically fit. The politics are gnarlier than the biology. New Mexico's early European settlers demonized and mythologized wolves—the Spaniards called them minions of Satan—and hunters are reluctant to share game with wild canids. For cattle and sheep ranchers, wolves tend to inhibit the cash flow by eating their investments raw. Nevertheless, studies of Mexican gray wolf recovery in the Southwest have defined a suitable site—suitable in terms of food (rodents, rabbits, ungulates), elevations (bajadas and mountains), and no overlap with livestock: the White Sands Missile Range.

"As far as I know, no other military base was asked to take on an endangered mammal in a recovery program," wildlife biologist Daisan Taylor told me earlier in our tour. "If we ever host the Mexican wolf here, we would put radio collars on them and track them and avoid denning sites during tests."

Wildlife recovery programs are often based on a habitat conservation plan, a strategy that would preserve an environment in which the animals could thrive. If, say, wolves roamed the military range and a Patriot missile clobbered one of them, the generals might not pay stiff penalties as long as the overall wolf population remained viable. However, the Army has rejected wolf reintroduction on White Sands on the grounds that the presence of *biologists* would interfere with its mission.

West of the missile range, on the Arizona–New Mexico border, the U.S. Fish and Wildlife Service did release Mexican wolves into a 7,000-square-mile "recovery zone" in the Gila and Apache National Forests. The wolves are collared and tracked. If they set one paw outside the zone or go within fangs' reach of livestock, they will pay a world of trouble.

The people who work at White Sands Missile Range take pride in the resident wildlife, a solicitude that is extraordinary when set against the nature of their work. (Physicist Ted Taylor described the noble infamy paradox well. Theoretical physicists involved in developing nuclear weapons, he said, constitute "a world of the best people and the worst possible results.") When military installations overlap wildlife habitat, four-leggeds seem to generate a comfortable, cathartic tolerance. Antelope will not raise the thornier moral issues of war or sell secrets to Libya. Bleached earless lizards do not pour blood on your file cabinets or handcuff themselves to your security fence.

Nevertheless, the military says it is not in New Mexico to preserve a gene pool of wild America. No one plans to turn the place back over to the slow hum of creosote evolution. Its environmental policies, the Army will tell you, present a kind of balance sheet: losses of habitat from military activities against gains made by restricting public access. These two million acres see no oil and gas exploitation or mining, few problems with overgrazing or the vandalism of archaeological sites, and no overtrampling by the Eden-starved pilgrims one finds stacked into national parks like cordwood.

I presume that I am expected to feel good about this BOMB IRAQ, SAVE A PUPFISH purview; about bombs that are not quite bombs but bomb*lets*; about the unprecedented postwar prosperity that has allowed us to even consider the well-being of bugs and bighorns; about how, in war, you save some peoples' lives by incinerating hundreds of thousands of others; about the lunch in my daypack, which, after a visit to ground zero, is probably radioactive. Hours ago, security wrote me off as a two-legged smudge on the grid who could not tell the difference between a quark and a flea's lip if I tried, so if I harbored any delusions about halting the defense establishment forever and turning this fawn-colored pelt of bombarded emptiness into a wilderness, I might as well give up.

Yet all manners of disturbing ironies surge forth—a desert as beautiful as it is terrible, its conflation of the sacred and the profane, the tension of the pure and sacrosanct against the penultimate human domination—and suddenly I am painfully homesick for my slickrock desert and on the verge of some kind of shameless and messy psychotic event on a top-secret military base inside this immaculate Army vehicle with two cordial hosts. I sit clumsily in the backseat. I feel as if I am their puppy. They try to tell me about an exceptionally rare falcon, one of the most stunning hunters in North America's avian tribe.

Aplomado falcons have been sighted in southern New Mexico and on the missile range. For years the closest birds were found in Veracruz, Mexico, Daisan Taylor says. Then several appeared farther north, at a ranch in the state of Chihuahua. The White Sands sightings may have been those birds, passing through.

"What would the Army do if it suddenly found itself the godparents of nesting aplomados," I ask, "herd the birds back across the border?"

"No," Taylor laughs. "They wouldn't chase off the birds. They would get rid of the staff biologists so they'd stop finding things."

When the bomb went off at Trinity, creating an intense flash of light that was visible in three states and noted by a blind woman fifty miles away, the Jornada's antelope were thought to have perished. The press later attributed their disappearance to the fiery explosion. Others said they bolted away on a frightened dash that did not end until they crossed the border into Mexico. Actually, a number of local antelope never lived long enough to greet the atomic age on that July morning. Military and test personnel had been eating them for months.

In late 1944 a small unit of military police established a base camp ten miles south of ground zero in preparation for the coming influx of workers. Supplies trucked into the remote camp would ultimately include, among other things, a steel tower; over a hundred tons of TNT; enough concrete to build six earth-sheltered bunkers; tinted welder's goggles to shield the eyes of test witnesses; two lead-lined Sherman tanks for retrieving radioactive samples after the test; white cotton surgical costumes for the technicians who handled the hot stuff; and cameras, lightbulbs, searchlights, batteries, generators, windmills, swamp coolers, buses, thirty-three dump trucks, an ambulance, a snowplow, a plutonium bomb, and a helium-filled test balloon named Barbara Anne.

The camp GIs dubbed their electrical works the East Jesus and Socorro Light and Water Company. The alkaline water from the desert's artesian wells covered their bodies with a film of minerals and made their hair stand on end. They were not let off base often, but they were allowed to hunt mule deer in the hills and antelope on the flats, for sport and meat, with rifles and submachine guns on safaris in jeeps and weapons carriers. The hunts put fresh meat on the mess table.

Tail gunners in bombers flying the Alamogordo Bombing and Gunnery Range strafed antelope with their machine guns for target practice. According to one account, military decree sanctioned the decimation of the antelope and any stray cattle that staggered into the gunnery range. Officially or otherwise, no one wanted a herd of freelance ungulates tripping over or entangling themselves in the intricate web of cables that radiated across the desert, among them the wires that fed firing circuits designed to rearrange the subatomic innards of an anxious globule of Pu-239. Other accounts claim that the antelope population survived, albeit in diminished numbers, that most of the pronghorn simply ducked under the T-poled wires on the run, and that at least one herd was spotted in the Jornada on the morning of the bomb. Since the war New Mexico's wildlife agency has introduced more pronghorn antelope

to the range. They graze free of competition with domestic livestock and dodge civilian bullets only when the Army opens portions of the range to special hunts.

As the date of the Trinity test approached, scientists were shut-
tled in from Los Alamos, swelling the camp's population to more
than four hundred, all men, few of them over the age of forty. The
barracks filled with mathematicians. The primary source of protein was antelope. An old livestock watering tank made a decent
swimming pool in the searing heat. Everyone's hair stood on end.
Today's better-coifed workforce lives far from this windswept
basin, in Alamogordo, Las Cruces, and other towns with lawns, air
conditioners, and golf. The primary protein source is pizza. The
ramshackle remnants of Trinity's base camp, which overlay an old
cattle ranch, are not part of the semiannual public tours, although
they remain on the inventory of historic properties.

We arrive at the old camp and step out of the car to explore.
Barracks, mess hall, stockrooms, makeshift labs, and windmills
have vanished. Nowhere in sight can I find a snowplow. Little
leaf sumac pushes up through the caliche. A derelict building
from the ranching era defies gravity, its sagging doorways choked
with tumbleweed, or Russian thistle, an exotic from Eurasia and
the only Russian invasion thus far into the secret heart of American defense. Empty windows gape toward Mockingbird Gap on
the horizon, barely held square by thick adobe walls that once
kept the interior at the cool, even temperature of a cave. Drifting
dirt, owl pellets, and rodent droppings cover the warped floor
planks, but the predominant scat was left here by oryx, also called
gemsbok—bulky, aggressive, and unlikely creatures of Africa's
Kalahari Desert, introduced to the Tularosa Basin in the sixties as
part of a program to serve up exotic big-game animals to sport
hunters.

If I were not ankle-deep in gemsbok poop, if I had no knowledge of the events that unfolded here between the winter of 1944 and the summer of 1945, between homestead and Hiroshima, this crumbling hulk would resemble the many other ghost ranches on western deserts and prairies given over to weeds and failure. Unlike the others, however, this place did not survive long enough to fail. It merely adjourned. It shared the map with a spindly tower, antelope, and a theory made into metal.

Long before the first detachment of military police arrived at this remote ranch, the Los Alamos scientists were certain that they could, without a test, deliver a uranium bomb, a gun-type weapon that fired one subcritical mass of U-235, an isotope painstakingly extracted from uranium ore, into another, creating a chain reaction. A precious supply of fissionable material went into a single bomb, whose dry run and war debut were one and the same: Hiroshima.

Uncertainties about the availability of enriched uranium led to the development of an alternative bomb that used plutonium. Implosion, the preferred method of firing such a weapon, squeezed from the plutonium a more efficient chain reaction than the uranium gun assembly. The implosion device, ultimately used on Nagasaki, had to be tested on a site that was secure, isolated, and within reasonable reach of its great "radiant brain," Los Alamos. The maps of the day offered the blankest expanses in desolate abundance.

In the old ranch house I kneel down to inspect the owl pellets scattered amid the floor rubble. The owl that roosted here coughed up these compact masses of indigestibles from its gizzard, and from the pellets come revelations. The menu du jour for owls at this ghost camp is rodent. I tease apart the dry, fibrous wad and uncover the tiniest, most delicate skull fragments, a shoulder joint, jaw, and limb bones as slender as toothpicks. It occurs to me that these bones and pellets, along with the sand and weeds, are the equivalent of the thick, fecund, vegetable invasions that swallowed entire Mayan cities over the millennia. Both desert and jungle seek some sort of equilibrium, at different speeds and densities. In the desert, unlike the jungle, few plants are strangled to death by their neighbors in a seizure of space; they are more likely to die of thirst. The desert's slow pace of recovery casts a thinner veneer over this monument. No scowling marble busts or lawns of facsimile trinitite embalm it.

Is geography fate? If I were not stumbling about the wind-blown Chihuahua with the miasmic dread of Trinity crushing my shoulder blades, I would bear the weight on San Nicolas Island, an outlier among the Channel Islands off the southern California coast, or on a sand barrier on the Gulf of Mexico near Corpus Christi, Texas. Isolated by water and easily secured, these islands made plausible candidates during the Manhattan Project's search for a test site.

Or I might be visiting Colorado's San Luis Valley, also on the list, in the shadow of the Sangre de Cristo Mountains and the Great Sand Dunes National Monument. Indian reservations, "virtually uninhabited" (except for Indians, of course), presented likely terrain but were spared by then Secretary of the Interior Harold Ickes, who scorned the dislocation of Indians from their lands. A tank and troop training area on the Mojave Desert near Rice, California, also fit the geography of foreboding uselessness, as did several dry valleys in New Mexico: the malpais south of Grants, broken mesa country near Cuba, and, near Alamogordo, the Tularosa Basin and Jornada del Muerto.

On any of these places one could hide things and make a fairly large, poisonous mess—impossible behavior in Boston or Virginia or amid the farms of Iowa, where people might notice one nuclear explosion, if not hundreds. Basin and range topography diluted the buffer of caution with its seemingly infinite and forgiving spaciousness, and for another four decades the West continued to provide suitable land for war games.

Some of the Trinity candidates—the unchosen—escaped; others did not. At Grants, New Mexico, uranium mines and a mill flourished as a postwar arms race churned out its "physics packages" (nuclear warheads). The Mojave Desert still harbors a lion's share of military reserves and, with facilities in the planning stages, could become the nation's premier nuclear waste dump.

Among the unchosen Trinities, their very allure as potential bombing ranges—their *wildness*—also made them attractive for preservation. The Texas candidate site is now part of the Padre Island National Seashore, home to North America's only breeding population of whooping cranes. Great Sand Dunes National Monument still rises above Colorado's San Luis Valley, and few visitors to this dazzling sea of wind and quartz crystals realize how history could have marked it. The Tularosa and Jornada del Muerto were sucked deeper into the military vortex, though not without their own distinctive bestiary of freeze-dried natives and Kalahari fantasies.

Add another few vertical inches of detritus and several more pounds of lounging gemsbok, and the shaky walls of this old building could easily collapse into a dusty heap. I leave before this happens, still bereft of any sense of human habitation. During the Trinity test the Jornada del Muerto was not *home* to anyone. It was a place where work was to be done, a hybrid of Boy Scout camp and war factory. As in the Hollywood westerns of my childhood, the morality play unfolded against a Wile E. Coyote backdrop. Here I am again in the scenery without explanation, looking for one, peering behind the stalwart heroes, around the dusty extras, trying to see what is there when everyone else already seems to know: "nothing."

Outside the adobe ruin the wind feels both refreshing and annoyingly turbulent. The indigo silhouettes of distant mountains deepen against a cloudless sky. So tangible is the earth's curvature, those mountains could at any moment slip down the ends of the arc and find themselves glued to the People's Republic of China. Winter light falls upon my immediate surroundings with a kind of vestal chastity unmolested by air or stratosphere.

Some people find New Mexico's famously lucent air unnerving and severe. Living in such clarity, they imply, is like living at the edge of the universe. When you put yourself in the bomb makers' boots, it is not difficult to see why they chose this particular edge of the universe for what was, on its face, a technical exercise. Here was a desolate void on which to stage a mesmerizing spectacle of engineering, the grand drama of abstract science made fire. If there was love here, it was not for this desert but for perfection, success, the splendor of man's handiwork. At this point the scientists' pragmatism and the momentum of their arduous labors reigned. Their invention had not yet wiped two cities off the face of the earth.

I seek the Oscuras again, the craggy rib of rock that reaches back through Cenozoic and Mesozoic to Precambrian times. The mountains loom above ground zero and its silly little remnants of steel tower, so dwarfed by sky, basin, and the central horror of an age. I find the escarpment and lock it in my gaze, aware that I bring to its otherwise indifferent beauty a perception tainted by ceremony, the imprint of human narrative on its stark contours of stone and shadow, as if such beauty must have to pay a somber penalty in sorrow.

Out from under the Cenozoic and Mesozoic, thoroughly aboard the Psychozoic, I am staring at the first 0.016 seconds of the nuclear age. In this freeze-frame photograph, Trinity's exploding star spews out atomic bits of itself in agitated torrents and with them drags humanity across an irreversible threshold. I am thinking that the cloche-shaped blister hovering over the night desert, an image caught by high-speed cameras as the bomb exploded, looks like a jellyfish. A breast. Or a zygote, the plump, fertilized union of two cells before it cleaves into a new individual through repeated mitotic divisions.

A set of black-and-white photographs of the explosion sequence is propped up against a wall at the McDonald Ranch house, one of the monument's restored structures, where I try not to sit on the floor for a better view because in 1945 the bomb's core was assembled in this room, and I do not want to get plutonium in my pants.

By a few seconds the swelling dome preceded the roiling fireball atop a thick pillar of smoke, the mushroom cloud that forever imprinted its doomsday self on human consciousness. Before dome or mushroom, of course, came an intense flash of light. It flooded the Jornada del Muerto with full daylight and blanched the face of the moon, and nearly every eyewitness recalled this "sheet of sun" as his most vivid first impression.

In the zygote photograph the luminous white hemisphere squeezes from its equator a skirt of turgid radioactive dust. It does not seem possible that so much heat could have so sharp and symmetrical an edge and, on the inside of the mass, the almost opaque density of living tissue or a marine organism.

In all of these photographs, including the detonation at its most mushroomesque, the ground is visible, if only as a dark horizontal footing. In contrast, the photographs of Hiroshima and Nagasaki, taken from the air, reveal slender, unearthly columns of smoke with no sign short of imagination of the holocaust beneath them. Fifty years later, that is still how we tell the story, in fragmented images and abstractions or in mantras of copious technical detail and meticulous analyses of historical context and policy making. For the warriors, who have the fewest illusions about the business of defense, the abstractions sanitize nuclear weapons. For the rest of us, they buffer despair, and it is human nature to seek them, to deflect the mind into something manageable, even bleakly comic, rather than face an unspeakable horror.

In their lenses the high-speed cameras caught equations transformed into energy then returned to numbers again—kilotonnage, temperature, pressure—that were Trinity's natal moments. For the semiannual open houses at the monument, these photographs are taken out of storage at the McDonald Ranch and hung on the chain-link fence that surrounds ground zero, not far from a replica of the steel casing that housed Trinity's twin over Nagasaki, a device that looks like a flatulent tadpole with a cheap, clunky wall fan for a tail. People want to see the symbols, the Army's Jim Eckles tells me when I ask him about the mood during the public tours. The statistics, the inert icons, the cenotaph of black rock— even the cathartic glow-in-the-dark jokes—endow ceremony to an event fraught with moral ambiguities but unequivocally clear about human mortality.

"The visits are solemn occasions," Eckles says. "No one knows quite what to do, so even though they aren't supposed to touch it or take any, the first thing they do is kneel down on the ground and look for trinitite."

At other times and places I have looked beyond numbers to the rest of the facts, as everyone should, because we are never free of the history of our home. Like the Trinity detonation photographs, the survivors' stories in Hersey's *Hiroshima* and Kenzaburo Ōe's *The Crazy Iris* replay nuclear warfare but from within, not beyond, *genshi bakudan,* "the original child bomb." They are replete with the ironies afforded to those who still have eyes to see the world once the horror has passed.

Burn patterns on the skin of Hiroshima women took the shapes of the flowers on their kimonos, where white repelled the bomb's heat and dark colors absorbed it. Some deep-seated instinct told a mother to bundle her children in heavy overcoats because she feared the *cold,* even though it was a hot August day and Hiroshima was on fire. For their first meal after the blast, a meal they could not hold in their bodies for long because of radiation sickness, several survivors ate garden pumpkins and potatoes that had been roasted on the vine by the bomb's heat. The panoramic photographs of Hiroshima after the bomb show nothing left of a city of seven rivers but seven rivers and an expanse of dust and rubble, all contours exposed. The first time I saw this landscape, I thought to myself, *It looks like a desert.*

The McDonald Ranch sits two miles south of ground zero, an adobe and stone dwelling built in 1913 by a German homesteader, then occupied by the McDonald family until the Army moved them aside for its gunnery range. The Trinity test blew out the house's windows and damaged the barn roof, and thus the place sat until the Park Service restored it to appear as it did in July of 1945, when a small team assembled the bomb's core in the master bedroom. My fears of a radioactive derrière are exaggerated. Back then dust was the enemy. "Please wipe feet," says the homely sign at the door, behind which two hemispheres of plutonium were joined, then transported to the shot tower.

Well before the farmhouse assembly, the Manhattan Project had passed from theory—"blackboard science"—to work performed by hand and tools. The Manhattan Project had been created to translate the threat of a Nazi atomic bomb into Allied hardware, and with Germany's surrender months past and a Pacific war yet to end, the hardware was nearly complete, the momentum unstoppable. By Trinity, said Frank Oppenheimer, brother of J. Robert Oppenheimer, "the machinery had caught us."

Other than placing themselves and rural New Mexico in the bomb's shadow, the Trinity team designed few biological studies. Precautions took the form of judging the safe distance between observers and ground zero, designing plans to evacuate nearby communities, and, if necessary, to declare martial law in central New Mexico. Monitors tracked the cloud of fallout as it sprinkled pixie dust over the Land of Enchantment. After the blast their studies were, to say the least, casual: they measured radioactivity, examined broken windows, and chatted with residents without spilling the frijoles about Trinity's secret test.

Only two experiments remotely addressed the weapon's killing power; both were thrown together at the last minute. On the day before the test, Frank Oppenheimer marked spots at increasing distances from ground zero. At each mark he set out pine shavings and boxes of excelsior and nailed strips of corrugated iron to pine boards. His constructions roughly simulated fragile Japanese houses. In another experiment a medical officer drove into the desert with a box of white mice, which he hung from signal wires by their tails. There they dangled with their upside-down view of the coming nuclear age. Before it came, the mice died of thirst.

Considering the Manhattan Project's complexity and manpower—130,000 people at geographically scattered labs and factories, in wartime conditions—it is a wonder, of uncertain blessings, that they reached this moment in a humble western farmhouse. Although reflection would come later, the men at Trinity first responded to their handiwork with a thought common to all big-brained, tool-making mammals since they lifted their knuckles off the ground: *It worked.*

"Some people claim to have wondered at the time about the future of mankind," said Norris Bradbury, who led the bomb assembly team and succeeded Oppenheimer as director of the Los Alamos facility. "I didn't. We were at war and the damned thing worked." Not only did it work, but no one else had one. American ingenuity remained incontestable until the Russians put together their own Fat Man in 1949. In those few years an oxcart-versus-automobile attitude would spawn jokes about the Soviets, who could not deliver an atomic bomb in a suitcase because they didn't know how to make a suitcase.

·   ·   ·

We leave the McDonald Ranch and head for Stallion Gate and tour's end, stopping briefly on the way to look over the remains of an instrument bunker of Trinity vintage. Concrete and mounded earth still reinforce a shedlike shelter. Most of Trinity's bunkers were bulldozed under or left to slump and crumble under the desert sky. Burying or exporting trinitite and other test artifacts to Somewhere may have addressed concerns about contamination from the blast or simply manifested a lack of interest in upkeep. As pressure to preserve the site bore down on the Army in the seventies, questions arose about the logistic tensions between running a restricted military base with secret, deadly, expensive stuff and operating a public monument wrought with the endless controversy generated by Trinity's paradox of greatness and infamy.

My hair blows east in the wind. I am weary of this wind and its straight shot across the playa into the side of my head. I wince in New Mexico's brassy light and the not altogether pleasant sensation of being too close to Texas. Against the distant bajadas stretches an olive-green swath of creosote bushes. In the foreground grows an island of soaptree yuccas that suddenly strike me as the silliest plants I have ever seen.

From a rosette of bayonet-shaped, gray-green leaves on the ground rises a thick trunk clothed in its own spiny sheath of brown needles, the leaves that die from the plant's base upward. Another burst of green spikes caps the trunk, and out of that shoots a narrow stalk of creamy flowers when the yucca is in bloom. The overall effect is of a dumpy-looking palm tree with its finger in a socket, Reddi Kilowatt lost in the Chihuahua. Smaller than its Mojave Desert cousin, the Joshua tree, the soaptree (*Yucca elata*) is more shrub than tree. Mixed with water, its roots suds up nicely. Southwestern Indians past and present use yucca soap for ceremonial purification. I once washed my hair with soap from the roots of narrowleaf yucca, one of the species that fills the yucca niche in my Colorado Plateau home, and it purified me from the backcountry haircut I had given myself with my Leatherman Super Tool and only a rain-filled pothole for a mirror.

My companions and I are surrounded by nordihydroguaiaretic acid, a reassuring counterpoint to any disobedient drones, errant cluster bombs, or foam-rubbery glops of solid missile fuel that might lurk beyond the borders over which the generals would consider me in trespass. This antioxidant, abbreviated as NDGA, is but one of many compounds bound up in the natural pharmacopoeia that proliferates basinwide in the form of the creosote bush, *Larrea tridentata*. On the flats of the Sonoran, Mojave, and Chihuahuan Deserts, from horizon to horizon, the creosote forest may be all that one can see. During a rain resins gather on leaf surfaces, then release their heady scent into the desert air.

The Trinity blast destroyed all vegetation within about a mile of ground zero. Creosote bushes were among the first plants to return. One particularly large specimen joined pop culture legends of twenty-foot-high yuccas, huge Hollywood ants swarming over family picnics like berserk Volkswagens, the socially challenged urban dinosoid known as Godzilla, and other postnuclear mutants, although gigantism occurs naturally albeit infrequently in creosote and yucca without the influence of ionizing radiation.

Once again I feel orphaned, unable, and, frankly, too paranoid to pursue the paths of my usual indulgent curiosity, the sensory explorations that might have me nosing about the blimplike yucca pods or rubbing creosote resin all over my body or seeking the insects that live in that feathery, aromatic bush, pretending to be plant parts—the females mimicking old stems, the males the young leaves. The physical confinement in so immense a space has strait-jacketed all senses but the lingering chill of a visit to ground zero. Divorced from my senses, I choke on an indigestible glut of history. When my hosts suggest lunch, I let them lead me off like a lobotomy patient.

"Arriving experimenters register here" says a sign near the building complex at Stallion Gate, the missile range's north entry and my exit from the Trinity tour. The cafeteria has a spare cleanliness and more pale-colored Formica than rational people should have to face. A number of experimenters have come in from the day's test—the explosion we had seen earlier from twenty miles away. Only one of the men dresses in military garb. The others wear khakis, windbreakers, and flannel shirts in avuncular plaids. After igniting several thousand tons of fuel oil and fertilizer in the desert, they work quietly on their cheeseburgers in a sunlit room.

I have spent the day in the warriors' world, which in the desert around us spawned the insensate logic of preserving the world by devising the tool with which to destroy it. In this work can be found all the elements of classical Greek tragedy, humankind's creation of the circumstances of its own entrapment. Yet for all I know, I may be looking at some of the tragedians who will ultimately dismantle the trap after a half century of "peace through mutual terror," people who will disarm the arsenal and design its tombs.

I brought my lunch, which I made in Santa Fe before I departed for Trinity at dawn, and which is now radioactive, stashed bravely in the pockets of my off-the-charts radioactive daypack, which sits on the floor beside my plutonium-encrusted shoes. I pull out a sandwich, a pathetic polygon of bread spread with some sort of New Age substance, and stare down at it. I feel a sudden aggressive benevolence toward everyone in this room, as if I could somehow set the world straight merely by goodwill, by doing the right thing—by being extremely *nice* to people. Instead I continue to stare stupidly at my lunch.

A few more sunshine units in my breasts will not make a big difference, I think. I was, after all, born to die. Ground zero lies seventeen miles over my right shoulder, perhaps filling with noisy ravens again. Since World War II—for much of my unrepentantly baby-booming life—our twenty-thousand-plus nuclear warheads kept me free and safe from someone else's twenty-thousand-plus nuclear warheads; they have denied this bloodiest of centuries its war number three. Fifty years of impending total planetary annihilation, and we did not die. I take a deep breath, mutter the requisite mantric antidotes, and prepare to lift up and bite into my sandwich.

Years ago, when I first became aware of an atomic bomb test near Alamogordo, New Mexico, my subadult mind combined polyglot images with imperfect information and formed them into an Event. My school history books "explained" Hiroshima by showing me pictures of Japanese officials signing documents of surrender—nothing to tell me that young girls like me, exposed within a half mile of Hiroshima's hypocenter, were seared to black char as their organs boiled away. The Atomic Energy Commission supplied my class with Dagwood Splits the Atom comic books as it routinely tested ever more powerful weapons on the sands of Nevada and gauged the effects on "doom towns" filled with families of well-dressed mannequins, who were "displaced" or "translated," in AEC jargon, if they were too close to ground zero: mother in her chaste shirtwaist and wicked stiletto heels, breasts aimed perkily toward her vacuum cleaner, father seeking curious spiritual oneness with his briefcase, eldest son with a cherubic benevolence I had never witnessed in my own brother, and a daughter like me but tidier and more resigned to a future of vacuum cleaners, about to get her ankle socks translated.

I knew of J. Robert Oppenheimer's directorship of the Manhattan Project and his teaching style at the University of California at Berkeley, where my parents were students before the war. No one could understand Oppenheimer or his physics, his students said, so they watched his cigarette intently—he smoked heavily—expecting him at any moment to write on the blackboard with it and smoke the chalk.

With this factoid salad in my head, I began to imagine Trinity.

There in some dark bunker, I thought, sat the gaunt and princely Oppenheimer, chain-smoking. Wires and cables swarmed around his ankles. In front of him a bulky console the size of a Chrysler glowed, crackled, whistled, and hummed. Needles jumped, dials whirled. He smoked, threw switches, twiddled heavy Bakelite knobs.

At countdown zero minus thirty seconds he hovered over a bulbous switch, which was wired to an automatic oven timer, black and white, just like the one my mother used to time her angel food cakes. Loudspeakers above his head blared a lilting waltz, a type of music that inspired, at its debut, a scandalous dance in which couples clung to one another, their clothes and hair flying wildly.

Oppenheimer lit one cigarette with another and crushed the butts into an overflowing ashtray. *Klock, klock, klock* went the oven timer. Beads of sweat broke out on his forehead and slid down his temples onto his shirt collar. At countdown minus two seconds *he definitely smoked the chalk.*

Now that the cold war and its four-trillion-dollar hemorrhage of the U.S. Treasury are over, now that decades of test data have been ingested into computer models, whose ground zeroes are cyberspace, not deserts, we eschew everything atomic but our salsa and our chicken wings. At the moment I am staring through my binoculars at one of the most impressive pieces of technology on the White Sands Missile Range, one that predates Trinity and may outlast any desktop warhead.

I drove north out of Stallion Gate, leaving, I would guess, the surveillance grid much as I entered it: a mobile blip of cheap paste. Once off military land I pulled over and parked the truck. I now sit atop its cab, looking back toward ground zero and listening to a tape of Tchaikovsky's Serenade for Strings in C, Opus 48, a waltz he claims to have written on an impulse, a piece characterized by critics as "northern Italian melodism."

Looming in the binoculars is an unlikely mound of earth near an old ranch site in the northern basin. The gently sloped mound rises from the flats to about two hundred feet, then levels off at its top. Although it appears to be the exact size and shape of a beagle tomb, this earthwork instead represents a pinnacle of desert technology, bred by the handmaidens of self-sufficiency and resourcefulness. According to local lore, the rancher routinely parked his vehicles on this humanmade hillock because their batteries were always low and it was thirty or more dusty miles to the nearest town and mechanic. When he wanted to drive somewhere he hopped into a truck, rolled it down the slope, and jump-started it.

I feel certain that I am well out of the range of the Army's scary projectiles, yet crossing my field of vision are two ground-based weapons the length and shape of Arabian scimitars. I push the binoculars into sharper focus. A pair of slender spikes that could, in a heartbeat, skewer a chorus line of overweight musk oxen are now heading toward an hors d'oeuvre: me.

On closer examination I dismiss them as tactical military hardware, recognize them as mammalian, and suffer a confusing lurch in geography. Last time I checked, I was still in New Mexico. Things, however, are beginning to look unusually African: flat, brushy plains, salt pans, windblown sand, patches of desert scrub, and, bearing the scimitars, *Oryx gazella,* a native of arid southeastern Africa commonly known as an oryx or gemsbok.

The gemsbok's black mane extends down a set of linebacker shoulders. Its tail is black and heavily tufted. Broad, rounded ears flare out from horns whose adult length ranges from about twenty-six to forty inches. Most of its pelage is sandy-gray with black on the face, legs, rump, and underbelly. To a lesser degree than stripes on zebras, the vivid facial and body markings of gemsbok break up their wearers into pieces, camouflaging them as they rest in the sun-dappled shade of low brush. None of North America's native or domestic ungulates have a face to match that of a gemsbok, whose style might be loosely described as sub-Saharan tribal Kabuki with a fetish for cosmetics. The white head bears distinct black patches on brow and nose. An elegant black eye stripe streaks up the pale cheeks. A gemsbok looks like a weight-lifting pronghorn antelope in drag.

Gemsbok feed on mesquite, a plant similar in form to their native acacia, and yucca, grasses, tumbleweeds, and other desert vegetation, often drawing their water requirements from their food. They mate year-round, but beyond that we know remarkably little about their population dynamics. Their horns can penetrate car doors and human femurs. Males spar with one another and, on occasion, with military detritus. One of the White Sands gemsbok immobilized himself with a parachute. The silk fabric covered his eyes and entangled his horns and front legs until he was tranquilized and extricated. A year later he turned up with pieces of another parachute in his horns.

Forty years ago the reasons for stocking the western wilds with gemsbok and other exotics had much to do with a lust for sport hunting, and little attention was paid to the effects of outsiders on the native biota. Abroad, and particularly in Africa, vast herds of big game appeared to rumble across the savanna, posing some unacceptable, world-conspiracy affront to the virility of the American male. In contrast, central New Mexico, with similar terrain and climate, was "empty." Sportsmen believed that places like the Tularosa Basin could support husky exotics in habitat niches unoccupied by natives. The idea was to import trophy species to game ranches, breed them, release their progeny into the wild, then stalk and shoot them.

State game officials purchased stock from private wild animal dealers, and, between 1950 and 1977, five species of exotic ungulates entered the New Mexico wilds, most by intentional release, a few by escape and unauthorized release. The southern deserts and mountains took on the bulk of the free-ranging exotics. However, one species, the Barbary sheep, a native of North Africa, ended up in northwestern New Mexico's Canyon Largo, which drains into the San Juan, my home river near the Four Corners.

In 1969 wildlife officials brought the first seven African gemsbok to the White Sands Missile Range and, for acclimatization and preliminary studies, placed them inside a fenced enclosure in a hilly canyon southeast of Trinity. The gemsbok promptly crossed the barbed wire as if it was dental floss. They moved directly to the desert flats east of the release site—habitat they obviously deemed more like the Kalahari—and began to populate southern New Mexico.

By 1973 game officials had released fifty-one animals on the White Sands Missile Range. By 1975 the herd had roughly doubled. None left the range's boundaries; life with the Survivability/ Lethality Analysis Directorate and the combat-induced obscurants of electromagnetic battlefield atmospheres was apparently a good life. No predators harassed or ate the gemsbok because there weren't any predators. In the late eighties the herd numbered about six hundred to eight hundred gemsbok, and some of them were visiting Texas to the east and wandering over to the Río Grande to the west.

Depending on whom you ask, the current population stands at eight hundred to sixteen hundred gemsbok, a broad and uncomfortably imprecise span of estimates. However, there is agreement on two things: wildlife managers need better surveys and studies, and gemsbok are becoming rather pesky around these parts, each one like a six-hundred-pound carp or starling.

The drag queen on the Jornada del Muerto abandons the temptation to toothpick me. It turns away and ambles off, leaving me to my waltz and the windblown emptiness. I pull out the Map of the Known Universe and sketch in ground zero, monkeys in space, pupfish, toads, a Russian suitcase, and generals in safari shirts and little white booties, shooting trinitite bullets at African oryx. I make a note to investigate the presence of a Saharan sheep back home in my neighborhood. I add a turtle on its back, remembering that Oppenheimer, on a walk in the desert after the Trinity blast, came across such a creature and knelt down to turn it right side up. The inky maze of lines on paper distracts me from the pair of cement shoes that seem to be strapped to my subconscious:

the luster of my goal—soothing a persistent spiritual malaise by a renewed closeness to nature—has been dimmed by further estrangement. All day I have struggled to read the desert in my usual manner, to discern its workings as they are mirrored by one of its creatures. I have tried feebly to turn Trinity's toads right side up.

If White Sands was not a missile range but a wilderness haven for backcountry recreation, if the risks of exploration were rattlesnake venom, dehydration, and one's own stupid mistakes rather than unexploded ordnance, missile ejecta, and certain arrest, brave nature seekers might sprint off through the yucca and muse about the insignificance of their own lives against the immutable sky and rock. That would be the right tack but the wrong epiphany for the naturalist's tour of the terrain of strategic death.

This haunted real estate is neither beautiful nor terrifying. It is beautifully terrible. It conflates the ultimate with the intimate, poises a strange equanimity between near-pristine lands and proving grounds for the extermination of life—a self-canceling proposition. It evokes a conflict of the psyche, a collision of dispassion and vulnerability, that may bear more veracity about our century's troublesome relationship to the western deserts than the most sublime nature photograph.

Monuments and artifacts carry the news of history in a kind of code of remembrance. Here at Trinity the land itself is the carrier—austere, at times bleak, a space so vast it absorbs all silences but its own. If no one tells you what happened here, nothing in the desert itself would give it away. The land appears to have no meaning beyond that which I bring to it with my own knowledge. Yet if who I am is geography as well as blood, if living where I do matters, then this place, too, is blood and home.

On the Map I draw lines from Tsé Valley on the Arizona-Utah border to Trinity, Hiroshima, and Nagasaki, piercing en route the flying rock with the big question mark. In this rock I sense the textured darkness of a connection, a physical link between Trinity's heart and the claret cup ledges. Like the African gemsbok and Barbary sheep in the great American desert, peculiar luggage has been checked into the Known Universe.

I pack up notebooks and drive back toward Santa Fe. Along the way I make a brief detour to the Bosque del Apache Wildlife Refuge on the Río Grande, winter breeding grounds for an astounding array of migratory waterfowl.

In *Hiroshima* John Hersey writes:

All day, people poured into Asano Park. This private estate was far enough away from the explosion so that its bamboos, pines, laurel, and maples were still alive, and the green place invited refugees—partly because they believed that if the Americans came back, they would bomb only buildings; partly because the foliage seemed a center of coolness and life, and the estate's exquisitely precise rock gardens, with their quiet pools and arching bridges, were very Japanese, normal, secure; and also partly (according to some who were there) because of an irresistible, atavistic urge to hide under leaves.

In February in New Mexico, there are few leaves. The best I can do on the Bosque del Apache, where over seventeen thousand sandhill cranes come to rest and feed among the reeds and marshes, is to lie back, *tséde* at last, on a cold stretch of winter earth, and listen to the pterodactyl-like cries of every last one of them.

Tsé Valley II:
Fossil River

In a fat black inner tube I float down the San Juan River, a river whose red-rock desert physique bears little resemblance to the ancient river that millions of years past ran through Tsé Valley, twenty miles to the south. The San Juan flows by my home and is so familiar, it is more bloodstream than place. Everything about it is tangible—a slick ribbon of jade silk between sienna canyon walls hung solid against a cerulean sky, pale sandy beaches, banks thick with lacy green tamarisk fronds, in which perch tiny gold finches. Everything about the Tsé River is invisible but inferable.

Like all rivers through time, the one in Tsé Valley meandered and braided, ate its banks, flooded, changed course, and changed course again. It was much larger than the San Juan—more like Canada's Yukon—and it was more than one watercourse, probably a complex interlacing of streams and tributaries that during the Triassic period wandered erratically across broad coastal lowlands (the "beach" was western Utah) following the path of least resistance. The ancestral Rockies, in what is now Colorado, sloughed themselves off into Utah and Arizona, and this river system carried them away and strewed them about the Colorado Plateau.

The gentle gradient of the coastal plains slowed the waters. The sluggish rivers dropped their sediment loads, and the future buried them. In that future, if you do not mind a whiplash-inducing rush through deep time, all varieties of geologic episodes rejumbled the landscape: encroaching seas, retreating seas, sand dunes, ever-thickening fluvial floodplains, mudflats, lagoons, swamps, more sand dunes, a great wrenching apart of North America and Europe, volcanoes, more continental drift, crustal deformations, orogenies, folding, faulting, igneous bulges, uplifts, down-cuts, some chilly glaciers to the north, and millions of years of weathering and erosion.

The San Juan is a young river, born somewhere back there in the bulges and downcuts. It established its principal drainage about ten million years ago, along with its parent river system, the Colorado. If I tubed another several days downriver, I would reach the Colorado River, a confluence now entombed beneath Lake Powell, the enormous reservoir behind Arizona's Glen Canyon Dam. Today I venture only the few miles between town and my land. Despite its youth, the San Juan can tell me much about Tsé Valley's fossil river. In my bulbous ring of somewhat stinky black rubber, purloined with monumental effort from a world that now runs on tubeless tires, I am stalking point bars.

On the Navajo side of the river—along here the San Juan is the reservation's northern boundary—a sandstone cliff rises six hundred feet straight up, roseate in the angled afternoon sun, with little but a narrow apron of boulders between its foot and the river's edge. The opposite bank is flat and gentle, thick with willow and tamarisk still full of busy finches. On a sandbar a great blue heron stares at me with a surprising degree of intimidation for what is essentially a smoky-blue wisp of a bird with a neck like a garden hose. To be fair, from its view I am an intrusion of drifting bipedal flotsam draped over a mobile black donut. I glare back at the heron and miss the tongue of deeper water over a gravel bar. Semisubmerged cobbles pummel my butt. Below the riffle I paddle over to a crescent of sand and extricate myself from the inner tube. I am standing on a point bar.

Point bars form on the insides of meanders; they are a river's sinuosity made solid. A river does not flow around a curve as an evenly broad sheet of water. Rather, the water rolls in a corkscrew motion. As it enters the bend, the river directs its strength into the far outside cusp of the curve with a scouring, erosive action that picks up silt and often shapes a steep, slightly concave cutbank. On the inside of the curve the current is weaker; there, the slower water drops its rolling load of sediment. Hydrologists call this crescent-shaped accumulation of solids a point bar.

On my point bar, baby tamarisk trees carpet the fine sand close to the water's edge. After spring runoff, tamarisk seeds sprout profusely on exposed sandbars, hellbent on creating a veritable forest of themselves. On the San Juan, as in much of the Colorado River watershed, God temporarily relinquished Her whims to the engineering schemes of advanced hominids banded together in a hydrocult known as the U.S. Bureau of Reclamation. Navajo Dam, over a hundred miles upstream, controls the floods in this basin. Without seasonal and significant scouring by large-volume, high-velocity waters, tamarisks tend to colonize the banks in weedy, greedy thousands.

At maturity the tamarisk, also known as salt cedar, is a prissy-looking, nonnative shrub decked out in feathery gray-green foliage topped by blooms of pale pink, lavender, or white. This finery belies the tamarisk's status as the control freak of the botanical world. Tamarisks invade then dominate riparian areas throughout the Southwest, their dense thickets squeeze big rivers into narrower channels, and they produce astronomical quantities of seed. Shed onto the ground, the leaves exude salt and create hypersaline soil conditions too nasty for other plants. Tamarisks send roots far down into the water table, then breathe groundwater into the air through transpiration at the rate of two hundred gallons a day. They can drain a small marsh in a few years. True haters of the tamarisk might drop to their knees and madly rip out every seedling from this sandbar. It would take six months and do no good.

Warmed by the sun, the inner tube releases gross petrochemical vapors. I abandon ship and walk inland. As vegetation increases its foothold, an exposed point bar will build up mud and sand and trap debris washed from upstream. I find twigs, bark, bits of conifers from the highlands upstream, leaf debris, cottonwood logs, and several specimens of the lower San Juan's most ubiquitous cultural artifact: yellow plastic Pennzoil bottles, commonly the quart size, emptied elsewhere (one hopes) of their motor oil. The yellow bottles are so profuse, surely their source is beyond random litter. As I thrash through a tamarisk thicket, I picture stolid, windowless factories built by Transylvanians and run by lobotomized but obedient executives from multinational petroleum conglomerates, wearing little yellow polypropylene jumpsuits and KGB crewcuts, disgorging this plastic rubble into the river by the ton.

The river that flowed through Tsé Valley during the Triassic period is now an entombed, waterless channel, but as a river it too had point bars. By Triassic standards, today's San Juan point bar entraps a motley collection of organics from an arid hinterland that grows bristly, thorny, scrubby plants with too much bare earth and blue sky between them. If I were tramping about the Tsé's river during the Triassic, however, I would be sweating under a languid, semitropical sun and slogging through ferny swamps or a dense forest with thick leaves and rotting dead things. If the humidity did not kill me, some manic, drooling reptile with pylon legs and a growling stomach the size of a small blimp might squish me like a bug in Tevas, then go straight for the black donut. In this fecund world, ancient point bars collected the lush masses of plant material that drifted downstream into their embrace.

Several million years and a lot of stumbling reptiles later, the forests vanished and the channel sands and gravels compressed into thick beds, the host rock for vegetable matter by this time carbonized in the old point bars. Into this environment, during another blip of geologic time, migrated a great deal more fluvial material and the molten matter and mineral-rich fluids associated with volcanic and igneous activities in the region. Ground and surface waters likely leached one of the minerals, uranium, through the porous upper rock strata until it reached the old riverbeds. There, the younger mineral concentrated in the organic debris embedded in the older Triassic point bars, forming rich veins of ore. In places the buried uranium and one of its secondary minerals, carnotite, replaced entire logs and plant beds.

Half a century ago mineral stalkers prized Triassic and Jurassic point bars far beyond routine curiosity. In Tsé Valley they sought the fossilized plant beds, guided to them by marker host rock, the Shinarump member of the Chinle Formation. They tunneled into these old riverbeds to reach the discontinuous pods of ore. They traded the grandiose spectacle of sun and desert for darkness and dust, leaving behind colossal red-rock spires, broken mesas, and the serrated ridgeline of Tsé k'aan.

Compared to geologic time—the time to go from fat, somnolent, Mesozoic rivers to a tunnel filled with human moles hacking up rocks—a half century barely registers. Yet it is this nanoblip that haunts me. Ever since my trips to the cactus ledges and to Trinity, I had wanted to find the date of the Tsé Valley mines. I now knew that date, and it was distracting me from an otherwise mindless downriver drift.

By the time I return to the inner tube and push off into the current again, the sun has dropped lower and I have broken one of my own rules about adventuring: to revel in the particularities of where I am rather than daydream about a place where I am not. Plenty of Earth history surrounds me, screams at me, reveals in its skin the planet's overwhelming inconstancy. Bodily, I am slipping down the exquisite, sunlit San Juan River, but my mind lingers on a single geologic metaphor: fossil river, specifically Tsé Valley's unimaginable, underground river and its dark, silent floor. I am nowhere in the here and now. I am tubing the Triassic.

When uranium is involved, you cannot simply float in an ambient curiosity about how various Earth forces put together and disassembled your neighborhood. Humans use uranium for bombs. As I sought the dates of the Tsé Valley uranium mines, I presumed that they had opened after World War II to fuel an ever-bloating cold war arsenal and countless nuclear tests in the South Pacific and Nevada desert. Research revealed that the mines had indeed contributed ore during the key years of Colorado Plateau uranium production, from about 1951 to the late seventies.

I also discovered that the Tsé mines had opened before the cold war. In fact they predated World War II and the Manhattan Project. In a somewhat plodding enterprise the valley's Shinarump outcrops surrendered carnotite, a mineral combination of uranium and vanadium, for its vanadium. Miners dug up pieces of the fossil river by shovel, stuffed them into sacks, and trucked them off to a processing plant, or mill. The mill extracted the vanadium and sold it as an alloy for steel production. The uranium, a by-product, stayed behind in waste piles. If for security reasons the government had not halted the sale of uranium in 1943, ore from those wastes could have been marketed for luminescent watch dials, medical treatments, a dye to tint glass bottles yellow, and one of the pigments (red-orange) in a dinnerware set glazed in hallucinatory Mexican jungle colors: Fiesta Ware.

Ahead the river splits around a sandy island. I must paddle over to the right channel so I won't miss the landing for the easy hike home. The lush emerald crowns of cottonwood trees mark the spot. Another heron stands on the tip of the island, a silvery fish in its bill.

Laws of nature can explain the motion of a heron's neck; they hold up the river cliffs and keep my tube buoyant but my body not. Somewhere out there intelligent people are reducing the birth of the universe to an equation. Those laws seduce us with their purity and precision, physicist Alan Lightman wrote in *Dance for Two*; scientific knowledge provides a reassuring degree of certainty. "Even Heisenberg's quantum Uncertainty Principle, which proclaimed that the future cannot be determined from the past, gave a mathematical formula for containing uncertainties, like a soundproof room built around someone who is screaming."

My approach pushes the heron downstream. It flies off, fish in its bill. History is whimsical, I think, and deliberately take the wrong channel around the island. I won't go home. I shall go deeper into the San Juan's heart. Poet Jim Harrison writes,

The river is as far as I can move
from the world of numbers

Manhattan Project histories list three uranium sources for the
world's first atomic bombs. Most of the ore came from the
Shinkolobwe mines in the former Belgian Congo and from mines
near Bear Lake in northern Canada. Early in the Manhattan Project the U.S. Army also dispatched an engineer to the Colorado
Plateau vanadium mills to take a careful look at dumps. In the
rubble lay paleolithic point bars and channel sediments that had
been quarried from mines around the region. The uranium in this
"waste" was now considered more valuable than the other minerals. An officially nonexistent team of physicists at an officially
nonexistent laboratory in New Mexico wanted all the uranium it
could lay its hands on. This strange course of human affairs wed
the Tsé to Trinity.

Learning to Find Home

From one of my natural history books I learn that side-blotched lizards are among the most difficult to noose. If I tie a Number 5 thread to a notched stick or telescopic fishing rod, build a tiny loop with knots and spit, and lurk about well-frequented lizard trails until a likely specimen saunters forth, with luck I might pass the noose over the unsuspecting little bugger's neck and jerk it tight. I am advised to carry my captives home in a muslin bag sewn with French seams. I am also to remember to keep them only as long as necessary for my observations. The author encourages me to "look upon them as though they have come to you for a holiday."

These consolations arrived too late for the young lizard that drowned in my coffee cup: I never had a noose, I do not know what the hell a French seam is. We might have shared the screen-house amiably, the lizard and I, as long as it obeyed my one rule governing domestic wildlife: no crawling up to the ceiling above the bed as I sleep and dropping on my face. Dead, *Uta stans-buriana* surrendered to leisurely scrutiny several concentrated inches of reptile anatomy, and ultimately I gave its pale belly the honored place on the Map of the Known Universe.

A map, it is said, organizes wonder. When I created mine, I had hoped to instill more deeply the desert aesthetic that year after year reflexively seduces me. From the most quotidian, instinc-tive details of my environment—light, seasons, creatures, textures, moods—I would draw a revelatory oasis, passion turned into something holy.

The Map of the Known Universe, however, *itched*. It did not stand still. Even though I had cast it over home terrain, it netted unsouled shapes and cruel angularities. I was convinced that foreign armies occupied the Known Universe. If you overlaid it with an opaque membrane, land mines—not cactus and buttes—would bump the surface and poke through. Old landmarks were decipherable but canted with new meaning. Herein lay famil-iar territory but territory husked and stripped bare, torn by fla-grant episodes of the unfamiliar. I wished to deny the Colorado Plateau's own history. I was ready for refuge. I was ready to stick the Map into the nearest sand dune and walk away.

A random outing for beauty had taken me to a serene and, to all appearances, immutable valley of rock. From there uranium mines barely twenty miles from the lizard's belly led me to Trinity, a monument yet engulfed by an incongruous geography of wilder-ness and industrial warfare. At Trinity I had discovered that my own neighborhood might be wired to the vortex of apocalyptic horror. This land to which I devoted my most fervent loyalty ran a gossamer tightrope between beauty and violence. I felt betrayed. My lover, my pure and faithful desert, was cheating.

Art critic Hermann Kern wrote that the center of a labyrinth signifies "the place and opportunity for a perception so fundamental that it demands a basic change in direction. To get out of the labyrinth one must turn around." Trinity had, I think, placed me in a labyrinth. I reeled about with toads, plutonium, and a world war in my pockets. To turn around, the next moves would require an entirely different musculature.

And so, during the spring that followed my visit to ground zero, I changed direction. I looked under the lizard's belly. I tried to find Home.

Lifeless and immobile, the little *Uta* had rested on the big paper map of the Colorado Plateau. Down the lizard's back ran keeled brown-and-gray scales speckled with faint patches the color of a robin's egg. In death the blue-black axillary patch, or side blotch, faded just as a fish's iridescent rainbow colors fade when you remove it from the water, gone before you can memorize them. Four tiny legs gently buttressed the slender body. The lamellae of its right hind limb—distinct scales on the underside of the toes— touched down on Shiprock, New Mexico. Directly beneath its ventral bulge lay zero coordinates, the plot of desert on which I lived. After Trinity, after that seismic ethical disturbance in the field, I denounced further nomadic compulsions and became a homebody. After Trinity these eight acres were all of the Known Universe that I could manage.

When the cottonwood trees were still lacy silver skeletons with tightly furled buds that fattened each day as if the tree roots fed them a steady diet of subterranean butter; when the sun rose each morning to a raucous chorus of coyotes and Canada geese, then gained enough warmth to lure into the open air flies, ants, freckles, and an occasional beetle, my husband, Mark, and I came to land with nothing more than four survey pins, and we fenced ourselves in.

We constructed sturdy corners and pounded steel posts into sand and hard-packed clay. We strung two strands of barbed wire across the top and hog fence, or woven wire, along the bottom, ending each day looking like pincushions with cowboy tans. Our act was quintessentially western and adaptive. It established "control" over a parcel of ground in a region whose innate aridity and lack of wood for fencing materials required a vernacular technology to define boundaries: thin strands of Bessemer steel woven around vicious barbs.

The fence divorced a rough rectangle from the adjacent ranch, a vast tract of rangeland along the San Juan River below us. The instant we bled over the final stretch of barbed wire and closed the rectangle, more than a hundred years of livestock grazing abruptly ceased. We began a reclamation of sorts. The fence penned us in. Outside, the cattle roamed, a mix of generic Herefords and semiwild, rangy-looking breeds that wandered in from "Across"— across the river on the Navajo side—and made themselves comfortable. The cattle, of course, had more land than we did.

Although regular employment would eventually make us weekend housebuilders, during that spring we had nearly a full month to work on the land. We moved ourselves and a camp kitchen into a simple frame structure with an aluminum roof, a raised plywood floor, and screen walls on all sides. The screenhouse had been destined for a dump when we claimed it. We dismantled it into panels and hauled the panels and their resident black widow spiders to our land, where we reassembled screenhouse and spiders beneath a canopy of cottonwood trees. Inside (a relative term when you

live with screens from ceiling to floor) Mark built a table and plat-
form bed. Until he shut off the windward corner with sheets of
plywood, the gusty spring storms, mostly rainless, roared through
the shack's open pores and blew the blankets off our bodies. Each
morning the sun rose directly in my eyes as I lay in bed, and the
cottonwood buds grew plumper. The geese made their noisy dawn
racket, defining a primordial stillness between honks, which I
strained to fill with the sound of the distant river.

While we strung the property line, a hired crew drilled our well.
The plan was to insert a long, expensive straw through top-
soil, layers of ancient stream cobbles, and a thick bed of Navajo
Sandstone to the artesian aquifer that underlay town and, we
hoped, our land a half mile from town's edge. I harbored no delu-
sion that this land could be restored to a purist's notion of pre-
Columbian wilderness. Nor did I wish to hypercivilize it with a
lawn and tedious snarl of tantrum-prone French perennials. We
were supplanting the cattle as interlopers with our own set of
imprints, but I did believe that, if we were careful, we could avoid
unnecessary catastrophe to the desert.

However, a ten-ton drilling rig does not have a fairy's touch.
Its tires stamped massive tread marks into the soft red sand and
crushed rabbitbrush and saltbush into fan-shaped roadkills. Jacked
up sixty-five feet from the truck bed, the derrick and drill looked
ready to suck up the entire Pennsylvanian and Permian periods
and supply Mobil with another oil field. Passing cars slowed down
to take a long look at this enormous steel tower erected over what
everyone thought was a cow pasture. There was nothing subtle
about it.

The well crew, three meaty men from another town, wore dark
shirts of some strangely hairy material topped by Hell's Angel
denim tattooed with spare testosterone. They grinned and scanned

the premises, looking to rebuild internal combustion engines or split a cord of pine with their foreheads or pull down a mule deer with their teeth. During breaks they knocked back six-packs of diet soda and pulled out their handguns from their pickup cabs to compare notes. Their hierarchy was congenial but firm: the one who knew the most about drilling wells was paid the least, they assured me.

At first they drove all over the property as if it was a dragstrip, crushing vegetation and murdering a delicate crust that would take another several hundred years to become soil again. When I raked away their errant tire tracks and reseeded the disturbed areas, they looked at me as if I had been doing sit-ups under a tractor. What they and their buddies did with environmentalists, the men explained, was Send Them Away. The ticket to Away, I presumed, bore some sort of relationship to the guns stuffed in their glove boxes amid tattered copies of *Golf & Ammo*.

I sympathized with their fears of change but not their assignment of blame. Like so many rural westerners who felt discarded and dismantled by the rapid growth and demographic upheavals in their region, the hard lurch from traditional to New West economies, they were seeking a target for their resentments.

Apparently the Colorado Plateau was crawling with couscous-fluffing, overmedicated, postdoctoral biomorphs. To prove it, the men brought me newsletters from the Sahara Club, a way-out-there group of off-road-vehicle enthusiasts, which warned that beating up environmentalists could be dangerous because "so many of them are homos" and "you might get splashed with AIDS-tainted blood." I conveyed my displeasure with this offensive nonsense by sauntering around their pickups' all-terrain radials with a Lady Macbeth sleepwalk and an ice pick. Thereafter, without a word, the drillers politely stayed on the main access to the well site. One of the men tried to make amends with a joke. "This Okie gets pulled over for speeding," he told me. "The highway patrolman looks into the Okie's car and asks, 'Got any I.D.?' The Okie says, ' 'Bout what?' "

Cold nights brought hard frosts to the screenhouse and froze the peach tree blossoms in town. The days grew warmer, however, and we wore T-shirts as we worked, surrendering more flesh to sunburn and scratch wounds. To spare the last innocent remnant of anatomy, my derrière, from wound or ache, I had to slap and beat my bicycle to dislodge the black widow spiders from beneath the seat before I pedaled into town. On a supply run to Colorado—the commercial center nearest to our Utah village was eighty miles away—I purchased more rolls of wire at the farm co-op and listened to the sweet peeps of newly hatched chicks for sale. I breathed the heavy scent of spring air in my clothes and ran my torn, blistered hands over the silken fur of a five-dollar rabbit.

For two days a windstorm pelted us with a hurricane of loose sand and plastered a wall of tumbleweeds against our gate. One by one I detached a dozen spiny globular plant skeletons, each like a barbaric loofah sponge and as light as a feather. The wind tore most of the tumbleweeds out of my hands, blew them thirty feet high in the air, and stuck them to the neighbor's fence across the dry wash or sailed them off to the rodeo grounds.

In the mornings Mark arose and fired up his chain saw before he had his coffee. What a man. In the evenings we hiked across the ranch bottom to the river and sat on its banks, too punctured and weary to do much but stare at the glassy sheet of passing water and the red cliffs that rose high above us on the Navajo side.

On the fence Mark wanted a taut stretch and posts strong enough to deter angry, lunging mastodons. I wanted to immerse my chapped pelt in a vat of lukewarm Jell-O. We pushed the fence line through the most difficult terrain, a dense thicket of tamarisk that Mark had opened with his chain saw for the final run of posts and wire. We tightened up the last strands and clipped them in place. All sides of the property were enclosed. The fence now circumscribed an intricate world.

Europocentrically our realm lies roughly 109° west of the Greenwich Meridian and 37° north of the equator, approximately the same latitude as Tunis and Bowling Green, Kentucky, the Ionian Sea, and the Tibetan Plateau. Hydrologically: the midbasin of the Pacific-bound San Juan River, which draws its lifeblood from Colorado's San Juan Mountains and drainages in the Four Corners region to its confluence with the Colorado River, there to contribute its bounty to the industrial farms and megalopolitan thirsts of urban Nevada, Arizona, and southern California. Physiographically: the Colorado Plateau Province, which sprawls between the Rocky Mountains and the Great Basin. Political boundaries define this place with typically overcooked linearity: a corner. It is southeastern Utah's claim to one of the Four, organized by county and tribal governments.

The county is nearly as large as Belize, and you will not find a single traffic light within its borders. The town has no bars, no doctors, no extra jobs. During a recent election only one campaign poster appeared, upside down on the chain-link fence that surrounds the rodeo grounds, next to a bolder, handpainted sign advertising FAT SHEEP. Desert-hardy churro rams mean more than votes, and if you really want to bargain you should speak Navajo. All the people here work hard and grow tired and sometimes feel as if they are getting nowhere. Nowhere—geographically speaking—is where a lot of us want to be. In this kind of place, one dreams about Paris, Singapore, or maybe a weekend in Phoenix, but stays put. The center of the world is elsewhere; the world has no other center but ours. No one is ever sure if we are hostages of isolation or the freest people in four states.

I inhabit a place where there is not much chance of being eaten by large mammals. So far the possibility of a golf course is slim. The popular media are action videos and pulp info-dramas dished out by satellite. Say "Kierkegaard" around here, and some of us might think you are choking on a walnut. In town a mix of cultures, an artistic bent, and an unexpected worldliness breed a loose-jointed tolerance. In the surrounding county, values fall into the category of ultraconservative rural western, underlain with Utah's insular Mormon theocracy. In the county seat the building that houses local government shares its town block with the building that hosts the predominant faith: the distance between church and state is precisely 34.5 feet. I inhabit a place where I must drive to another state for a screw, and where, when I get to that state, go to a liquor store, stand before a decent selection of wine, and start to sob, the proprietor says in a voice sodden with pity, "You're from Utah, aren't you?"

Around here data have not yet outrun meaning. We have no onramp to the information highway without rigging special transportation circuits powered by a limitless supply of hyperactive pocket gophers. However, we do have the world's only shrink-wrapped Winnebago: a vintage recreational vehicle stuffed snugly into an inflatable Quonset hut.

The predominant language in the laundromat is not English but an ancient Athabaskan tongue, and the town scourge is not the officious gargle of cellular phones ringing in people's pants but an unrepentant plague of goatheads: *Tribulus terrestris*, "tribulation of the earth," a puncture vine with vicious spikes, no manners, and a sadistic appetite for bicycle tires. Under the lizard's belly I surrender to a nature more feral than civilized and do not care that I am this way because everyone else is wildly eccentric, too, and would not give a hoot if you wore your pajamas to the post office, which I did, once, stylishly under a jacket, with mud-caked river sandals, chatting away with one of my elderly neighbors, who had mounted on his bicycle's flask holder not water but a can of Fix-A-Flat.

The earth my husband and I occupy lies about five hundred miles from Trinity ground zero, on one of the Colorado Plateau's stacked plates of sedimentary rock. It is a desert but cooler and wetter than the Chihuahuan, and, on these eight acres at least, toads are scarce. Rain is a notable event. During one terrible drought, when the first rain in eight months fell just before dawn, everyone in town rose from their beds, rushed outside, and stood in the dark, palms upturned. The summer heat can turn the leaves on your garden plants into potato chips and melt the contents of your cranium out your ears. The winter winds carry a frigid sting and a concern about your Navajo neighbors Across, many of whom live without power or running water.

Navajo cartography, the maps of my neighbors, merges metaphysical with physical boundaries. They place me inside a vast region held within the circle of four sacred peaks that were breathed into life long ago, assigned light and color, and inhabited by gods: Sisnaajinii, Tso'dzil, Dook'o'ooslííd, Dibé Ntsaa—four mountains in Colorado, New Mexico, and Arizona. If I had on our land a very tall flagpole and I climbed to the top, I would see Dibé Ntsaa, ritualistically girded in black jet, fastened to the earth by a rainbow, and bathed in darkness.

Within their world the pastoral Navajo spread themselves thin— often separated by the vast acreage of a family's sheep allotment— instead of packing themselves together in villages as Pueblo farmers past and present have done. Both of these topographic occupations fit this high-spirited, sweeping space under the dome of heaven.

Astronomically, I try to use my home beneath the lizard's belly like a calendar. I calibrate the course of the seasons by marking the points of sunrise above the river cliffs, the movement of amethyst shadows cast by distinct columns of sandstone, and bloodred winter sunsets flung from the place where, it is said, the skin-walkers concentrate. I hide or throw away clocks and watches, convinced that if we are to choose the more sedentary, farmer stance in the Known Universe, we should, like the Hopi to the south, hold fast to our horizons and have the gods help us here.

My geography savors a delicious paradox: Home—a grounding—found in unearthly beauty. Here, for the past several million years, most of the earth's topmost layer has blown or washed away and what remains are voluptuous rises of sandstone and spare, stripped-down, standing-up rock that looks like red bones. The predominant colors are blue, emerald, and terra-cotta. Every day, every season, I taste these colors and the intricate flavors of their uncountable tones and hues. I have yet to earn this land. Perhaps I never will. Home is like religion. Sensibly you understand the need for it, yet not even sensible people can explain it.

In Utah, God wants you to have a lawn. An unkempt, weedy yard around a house can mean only one thing: the person inside is dead.

Where I live is an anomaly—there are few formal lawns. The church, the school, and several homes sit on rectangles of green chives that appear to be groomed by fleets of mute gardeners wielding the busy scissors of tiny, red Swiss Army knives. Everyone else wrangles drought-tolerant grasses and an *intifada* of goatheads and motley weeds. People nurture shade trees, heat-tolerant flowers, perhaps a tomato or corn patch and some wicked chiles destined for the year's most conflagrational salsa. A lawn is based on the principle of overcoming rather than adapting to local conditions. Here, however, lawnlessness is not a shirking of one's religious duty to conquer bestial nature. It is adaptive realism.

I looked at our desert plot as a kind of slut's Walden Pond. It retained its unruly character by sheer defiance and lovable perversity. Its aesthetics came not from the vanity afforded by moister climes but from narrower margins of survival. I was not its gardener but a kind of avocational meddler, an enthusiastic member of what I liked to call the Saint Thomas Aquinas Cactus and Succulent Society. Adaptation to this landscape required the eye of the vacant-lot ecologist: alertness to rapid change, rogue opportunists, and kinetic reclamation. The place was in the act of reforming itself, biologically intractable but not "wild." Plenty of that—undeveloped, sparsely populated desert—lay around me in abundance. I considered it, too, an intimate part of my home.

The world inside our fence straddled an ancient, sand- and shrub-covered river terrace, then sloped down to a cottonwood grove and grassy pasture. The land appeared raw and shaggy, strangely ascetic. The most obvious and recent ecological imperialists were cattlemen, the invasion of exotic plants, and the floodless floodplain, deflooded for the past three decades by the big dam and other waterworks upstream. Vegetation clung to the bench, manipulated by cycles of moisture and drought and the palates of domestic herbivores. Tumbleweed, cheatgrass, and snakeweed indicated a long history of disturbance and overgrazing, and hairy, thorny, aggressive proof that nature abhors a vacuum. Botanical scum that they might be in the eyes of purists, without these vigorous invaders further erosion would gnaw the slope into a mass of gullies and scour the bench to dust.

Disturbed or "natural," a plant community is a dynamic entity, constantly responding to environmental changes, some abrupt, others so subtle and long term, Mark and I will not live long enough to witness their effect. Our fence precipitated a radical change in the local plant ecology. As our tenure began, the land entered a weedy sere best described as Unchewed.

Wildlife with a preference for shrubs and forbs and open skies lived on the bench: black-tailed jackrabbits, lizards, raptors, bullsnakes, antelope squirrels, flycatchers, a trio of unreconstructed well diggers, and two ravens dubbed Heckle and Jeckle, who perched on the fence posts demanding watermelons or some such bribe for their pretending not to notice our folly and for our blessing of their unquestionable superiority. The cottonwood grove sheltered screenhouse, whiptail snakes, songbirds, pheasants, and a narrow riparian strip created by groundwater that surfaced into a small drainage ditch. The water attracted butterflies in summer. I often looked for toads there, too.

Of the three ecotones—bench, cottonwood grove, grassy pasture—the pasture changed the most dramatically once the fence went up. On the cows' side of the barbed wire, the pasture retained its buzzcut. On the no-longer-grazed side, stubs of bunchgrass quickly grew into shockingly lush, breeze-swept shafts as high as my shoulders. The fence marked a seam between what looked like two demo plots. This lack of husbandry on Unchewed bothered our more utilitarian, tame-the-wilderness neighbors. Get some heifers, they advised. Get some horses. Get out the Agent Orange. But until the imminent collapse of the techno-industrial state, when we would need the land to grow our own food, I was curious to see what the next sequence of botanical anarchy might bring. If healing my estrangement from Place meant bonding with weeds, then so be it.

Beyond the property two spectacular escarpments of sandstone, Triassic rock overlaid by younger Jurassic, held the valley in their embrace. The river and my inner-tube route flowed at the base of the southern cliffs, forming the boundary between the United States and the Navajo Nation. One entered the valley at either end or through a slot in the northern cliffs, a slickrock canyon with deep-set, high-ceilinged alcoves tucked under the rimrock.

Unless it scuffs up your shoes, few people take serious note of the bedrock that underlies their lives. Around here bedrock—inert as well as friable and movable—is the main event. This seemingly immutable landscape spends much of its time coming apart. The earth beneath the lizard's belly is aeolian and fluvial, shaped by wind and water, namely, the river and the ephemeral washes that feed it. Everything loose on those cliffs that wants to come down to valley and river does, and we lived atop it. Over the millennia the wind rearranged these deposits into a vast dune field.

At first glance you see rolling desert. Mentally peel off the scant plant cover, and you will detect the distinct contours of aged but still active dunes. Longitudinal dunes stretch out and streamline in the direction of the prevailing winds. Sand that piles up against a cliff face in a reverse cascade, looking as if it would like to climb it, bears the Dadaist name climbing dune. Sand that blows over a cliff and down the side is a falling dune.

Mounds of sand known as coppice dunes accumulate beneath the greasewood shrubs scattered about the terraces. The private life of a coppice dune involves deflocculation, the dispersal of clay in the soil around the plant, and chemical interactions that harden the soil to a concretelike mass not easily penetrated by water or excavated by ants. The clay pan remains as a conspicuously bare ring long after the greasewood bush dies and disappears.

The fifth type of dune around here is parabolic, a young, crescent-shaped dune with a windblown depression at its center. A herd of parabolic dunes marched along one border of our land.

Normally I would not impose something like deflocculation on anyone. However, in these two very localized soil formations—coppice remnants and parabolic dunes—could be found an adobe hearth of one of the only houses that preceded mine on the home bench, and the burial of eighteen men, women, and children at the end of my driveway.

In New Mexico's Jornada del Muerto the handful of cattle wranglers who preceded the atom wranglers filled their cups and stock tanks with the basin's subsurface water. Heavy concentrations of sulfates and salts rendered the water hard and filmy, attributes that evoked complaints about washwater during the time of Trinity and conjure, for me at least, this image: mad scientists with wacky hairdos—strands spiking straight up toward the ceiling fixtures like thin stalks of sheetrock—trying to blow up the universe. The early wells on the Jornada were shallow and artesian. What Mark and I wanted on our patch of desert was a less saline artesian well—that is, water tapped from deep rock layers, with enough hydrostatic pressure to keep it flowing without pumping it.

Naively I envisioned our aquifer as a kind of stop-action amoeba, an amorphous shape formed by its own flowing motion, with new, limblike pseudopodia extended outward and old ones retracted into the main plasmic blob. I feared that the well diggers' drill would miss the main blob or strike the empty bays between the liquid pseudopodia, and we would end up with a dry hole. The drillers would not listen to anything remotely amoeboid. We will hit water, they reassured me, the well will be artesian. The variables were depth, pressure, and hairdos.

To denizens of more humid places, nothing about this austere landscape hints that water even exists beyond the paltry amount that falls out of the sky or flows downriver to California's swimming pools. Strangers see acre upon acre of spotty, scraggly plant dwarfs, desiccated soil, and locals with faces weathered like handbags sewn from the skins of rare crocodilians, slugging down ice water as if they lived in hell.

My desert is land held together by hidden water. It descends slowly through giant tanks of porous sandstone and emerges as seeps and springs scattered in the nearby cliffs. Closer to the river you can trace the water table in places like our cottonwood-tamarisk grove. It rises up the roots of the venerable cottonwoods in town and nourishes the leaves that shade us from summer's heat. Mark and I depended on the subsurface aquifer, which had supported the tiny community for more than a century, to feed its precious fluid into our small straw as well.

Mark strengthened fence corners. The drillers drilled. I flitted about with my rake, scattering Indian ricegrass, blue flax, penstemon, and other seeds. The wind blew soil and seeds to Colorado. At night we staggered up from the screenhouse to stare stupidly at the well works and to listen to the wings of nighthawks carve the air. The tower gleamed in the moonlight, its steely probe aimed resolutely for downtown Beijing.

Nearly every day, people stopped by to examine the operation and troll for gossip. One of them was an older neighbor with a walk so disjointed, he seemed held together by duct tape. He had worked heavy machinery all his life, including a stint as a trucker hauling uranium ore from mines to mill during the cold war boom. For this man and many of his contemporaries, the passing of that era was the region's great tragedy. They clung to 1955—or to whichever year that life had last made any sense—with all their might, to the hope that uranium's Second Coming might rescue them from the New West's bed-and-breakfast economy and other unmanly endeavors. The uranium boom brought prosperity to their backwaters. It elevated the self-made man and his sense of control over women, children, and big-game animals. It built roads, schools, utilities, and a colossal myth.

The myth portrayed the Colorado Plateau miners as a wholly independent lot, free to be enriched or broken by their own labors in a free market. An entrenched hatred of federal authority and "creeping socialism"—still simmering today—denied the fact that uranium production was the tightly reined progeny of unabashed government paternalism. For years the Atomic Energy Commission, uranium's sole buyer, ensured a market for ore by requiring big company mills to purchase a certain percentage from independent prospectors. The AEC guaranteed prices and subsidized access roads, mine development, and other services. Although you would never hear it from the lips of rugged individualists like my neighbor, the dreaded feds, prodded by the frenetic arms race with the former Soviet Union, "welfared" the uranium miners in every respect but their health. (Mine safety regulations were nonexistent or ignored.)

The uranium-era good times still nourish a nostalgia so sweetly sincere, it could climb out of a glass all by itself. Around here we *like* the boom-and-bust economy, a county official told a journalist, although others may fail to see the pleasure in jobs lost, houses impossible to sell, vehicles repossessed, families uprooted and relocated, scary messes left behind, and no one to take responsibility for cleaning them up. The same officials court private and federal endeavors to store high-level nuclear waste in the county, reasoning that because the uranium came out of this country, it is the county's patriotic duty to "put it back." They consider the difference between clumpy chunks of ore and extremely hazardous weapons waste and spent nuclear reactor fuel to be irrelevant.

The uranium rush in the fifties left airstrips atop remote mesas

and roadcuts up and down steep talus slopes. Broken machinery
and scattered heaps of core samples still litter hauling depots and
abandoned mine shafts. The old camps tremble with the ghosts of
women who accompanied their miner husbands to the rugged
canyon country and lived year-round in empty silence and burning
rock, sand up to their ankles and a lumber and tarpaper shack
built by the miners for the cost of seven cases of beer. On a hike
into an isolated stretch of desert near the site of an old Colorado
River ferry, I once came across a parked Hudson, late-forties vintage, intact and cannibalized only for its tires.

During my neighbor's visit to our land, we watched the drill
bit pound its way underground to the aquifer. He leaned on a
shovel and with astounding simplicity told me how to make an
atomic bomb.

"You pack your Pu-239 into a tight ball," he said, making a fist.
"You got your neutrons and protons and your gammas all
together, jittery. Then you . . ."

"Throw it in the blender," I added, hoping to thwart this disturbing trend in gourmet physics.

". . . send a shock through it and let the neutrons go flying off.
The chain reaction begins in the nuculus until so many neutrons
are hittin' the other neutrons, you have a big explosion. And that's
the Bomb."

Late on a warm afternoon not long into the drilling operation,
the crew reached the aquifer. They cased the upper section, then
extended the line deeper, tapping the best water. When they finished, they packed up their tools and drove the drill rig off the
work pad, unveiling a patchy waste of sand and grease. Two feet of
steel pipe poked out of the red sand and turned an L bend capped
with a bright blue valve. Out of this pipe flowed an ungodly liquid
the color of tomato juice.

"Pressure's good," the crew boss told us, wiping his hands on an oily rag. "You've got one of the best wells around."

I stared grimly at the world's most expensive subterranean vegetable drink, wondering if it was perhaps a good time for me to be Sent Away.

"Let it run overnight," the crew boss said.

I did not sleep well. Several times I left our bed and visited the wellhead, tempted to shut off the valve. Never did my desert bones allow me to take water for granted. Running it this way seemed profligate and insane. I sat under the Milky Way's broken necklace and watched the pipe spew artesian ketchup. I pictured Mark and me forever dressed in a sad, tomato-colored wardrobe, our clothes laundered in red water.

We awoke to warm sun on our faces and the ecstasy of a future without fence building. The buds on the cottonwoods were obese, ready to burst into new green leaves before our very eyes. While Mark made coffee on the Coleman stove, I dressed and walked up the bench to the well.

I had lived in the desert long enough to know that the waltz of survival is danced with two partners: the desert's water and your life. Fatal thirsts, Mary Austin wrote of Death Valley in *The Land of Little Rain*, often arose out of a person's ignorance of concealed water, marked by the desert's own visage, if only one knew how to read it. The ill-equipped traveler who sought potentially unreliable springs and creeks could end up facedown in the sand, tongue two feet above a shallow, subsurface water pocket. "It is this nearness of unimagined help that makes the tragedy," Austin said.

Our realm was no Death Valley. Nor was it the Jornada del Muerto, strewn with the ghosts of sun-dried Spaniards. I had no doubt that we would quench our thirsts nicely beneath the lizard's belly. Nevertheless, our tenure here required a substantial gift and the humility to know that it was temporal, and far less enduring than the fact of aridity itself.

Out there in the rest of the Known Universe, too, there seemed no better guide than water. I knew only one way to penetrate the surface and learn anything from those larger increments of territory: apply the instincts of Home, look for the "nearness of the unimagined."

In a few months, if we did not shade the steel pipe with a wellhouse, summer's sun would heat it and its liquid charge to scalding. That would be another day. On this morning the spring sun shone with gentle somnolence, the cottonwood leaves could not be rushed, and out of the pipe flowed cool, clear water with the unwavering purity of ice.

The days of my town dump are numbered. It is a deep pit, landfill-style dump surrounded by a thousand acres of open desert with a view well into the next state. You can spot the dump by a plume of smoke or a scattered confetti of jet-black ravens and airborne bits of paper and plastic.

The county will soon replace this dump with a transfer station. Instead of dirtballing down the rutted access road with our motley loads, we will drive up a well-graded gravel ramp that leads to a tidy row of Dumpsters, into which we will drop our tidy bundles of garbage. When the Dumpsters are full, trucks will haul them to a landfill to the north—also in the middle of the desert, with ravens and plastic and a million-dollar view. For a fee, this dump will collect any dead animals we happen to discard: ten dollars for a dead horse, two and a half dollars for a sheep.

The old dump is a mess. Most of us are quite fond of it, especially now that it is destined to be a mess no longer. Gusty winds blow plastic sacks all over the desert, where they have not quite begun to biodegrade. The old dump is always on fire. The smoke rises thick and black behind the "No Burning Allowed" sign.

On quiet days a heap of charred cans smolders in the pit. You park, walk a minefield of diapers, then pass mattresses exploding their inner fluff, hulks of old washing machines, and a large, possibly toxic sofa. You resist the pathetic, starving puppy that some jerk abandoned amid the instant-pudding cups. You also resist taking a peek at the address labels on the mail-order sex magazines scattered among the crushed Cheerios boxes because you do not care to know which of your neighbors subscribes to such crap. Then you edge up to the lip of the fiery pit and test the heat. If your sneakers melt, it is probably not a good day to scavenge.

So far nothing at this dump has surpassed the finest treasure I ever scavenged. At another time, from a different small-town landfill, I once plucked my prize: a red velvet swimsuit. The black bears that raided the open pit at dusk had not yet shredded it; no ectoplasmic garbage muck had sullied its lush fibers. The fifties-style suit was in mint condition—vintage Esther Williams, barely worn, a perfect fit. Obviously no woman had dared swim in that suit, nor did I. A florid collusion of polymers plastered it to the body like blow-dried vinyl. A pair of curved velvet bowls the size of inverted Dream Whip containers announced my breasts. Although I seldom wore red clothes, how could I resist the fervent naughtiness, the martyred harlotry, that smoldered in that Egyptian whorehouse red?

Because we live many miles from the nearest store, people in my town save and reuse nearly everything. When we finally haul something to the dump, we are not convinced that its life has truly ended. By unspoken agreement we segregate our ambivalence. Gross undesirables like kitchen garbage go on the pyre. Furniture, appliances, and scrap lumber are set aside so the next person can look them over, perhaps remove some screws or nails or recycle a wire or turn a chair leg into a stake for a tomato plant.

No one knows when we will change from the old dump to the new system. When the change comes, there will no longer be an ambivalence heap. We will have to bite the bullet. We will have to drive to Colorado or New Mexico for a screw. No one will miss the smoldering pyre, and, when the wind blows, no one will miss the plastic stuck all over the greasewood bushes. We shall see the end of polite scavenging. We will never know who bought a new sofa and cast out the old, who gut-shot their TVs, or who gets the sex stuff. When the old dump closes, when the debris of our lives falls into the chasm of a tidy steel box behind a chain-link fence, we shall know a lot less about one another.

In the fifties and sixties the town dump sat at a different site, closer to the river and exposed in the carefree manner of an era with less volume of ooze, plastic, and conscience. People drove to the edge of a gravel terrace and tossed their loads down its natural talus. The slope still glistens with broken glass and chunks of eviscerated vehicles. Not much else remains but rusted metal and the petrified licorice of old tires baked by the desert sun.

By far the oldest dump in the neighborhood is a trash midden dating back to about the sixth century or earlier. It too collected household rejecta, which amounted to charcoal, ash, ceramic vessels and sherds, stone tools, maize cob fragments, animal bones, and dead people. The midden belonged to a group of resident Anasazi Indians, a name broadly applied to the aboriginal cultures that occupied this region from about 1500 B.C. to A.D. 1350. The Anasazi often buried their dead in midden heaps, placing the bodies in shallow graves with personal possessions, a few offerings, or nothing at all.*

Wind and erosion entombed the sixth-century midden under a parabolic sand dune at the end of my driveway. In it were bits of birds and animals quite familiar in the Known Universe and the skeletons of eighteen of my predecessors on the bench above the San Juan River.

To order the ancient southwestern world, archaeologists use a chronological framework defined by distinct material traditions and approximate dates. On the earliest end of the chronology, possibly as far back as 9500 B.C., are Paleo-Indian peoples—broadly dispersed, highly mobile hunters and gatherers. On the later end of the chronology, about a thousand years ago, are bean and corn farmers who lived in elaborate masonry villages such as those in New Mexico's Chaco Canyon, and the cliff dwellers who tucked their multiroom pueblos into the Colorado Plateau's numerous canyons. Though uniquitous and intriguing, this late Pueblo era was one of several cultural phases that ended when the people moved out of the region and aggregated into Hopi, Zuni, and Pueblo groups along the Río Grande.

---

*Let us pause a moment to pummel our lips. The name *Anasazi*, an Anglo mongrelization of a Navajo word roughly translated as "enemy ancestors," may soon disappear from the southwestern lexicon. Contemporary Pueblo Indians, who are the Anasazi's descendants, consider the name mildly insulting and prefer their own words—*Hisatsinom*, Hopi for "ancestors," for example. With the approval of modern Puebloans, archaeologists and anthropologists have begun to use a less tribe-specific term: *Ancestral Puebloans*. The trade is the image-loaded albeit prickly word *Anasazi* for due respect and a mouthful of styrofoam packing nuggets.

Say it quickly: "Ancestral Puebloans." Try not to die of boredom halfway to the *-stral*. Challenge your local poet to use it in his or her next work.

While the objection to *Anasazi* is legitimate, we are all likely to slip into comas before *Ancestral Puebloans* takes hold. Therefore, no disrespect is intended as I wean myself from the older term.

The human presence on our stretch of the San Juan River was continuous, if not erratic, from hunter-gatherer to late Pueblo times. Along that timeline the midden and several nearby habitation sites are classified as Basketmaker III, an Anasazi period (A.D. 500 to 750) whose cultural traits include basketry, simple pottery, the addition of beans to corn horticulture, and an increasingly sedentary life, usually in semipermanent villages near river or stream bottoms. The Basketmaker III settlement in my neighborhood was occupied from about A.D. 500 to 600.

Laid end to end, the volumes of material written about these early southwesterners would reach from here to Trinity ground zero, and they would include the finest field research and ethnological studies. Beyond academia, the Anasazi have also become America's favorite prehistoric people. Every year thousands of aficionados visit the meticulously restored and protected pueblo villages at Mesa Verde National Park, enjoying a domesticated, drive-by Anasazi experience. No one leaves the Southwest alive without a petroglyph T-shirt. No emissary of myth reaches across the dust-choked millennia quite like the thoroughly redigested figure known as Kokopelli, variously depicted in prehistoric rock art as a horned, humpbacked anthropomorph with a flute and an engorged penis, but now available without the penis on charm bracelets, lampshades, nut dishes, pajamas, and cocktail napkins. The oldest Puebloans have become cult-skewered, marketable icons, drained of reality based on the actual lives of Native Americans, past or present. Modern fascination with them is symbolic, some speculate, of a society so indentured by materialism, it aches for "earthy" knowledge and spiritual enrichment.

Let others fathom the Anasazi's peculiar entry into the global economy. I invite you to explore the respected works of southwestern prehistory and, if you must, hold your notes down with

the penisless paperweight statuette of a five-iron-swinging Kokopelli, who ought to be dubbed Golfopelli, sold by a popular mail-
order company. In the meantime I would like to examine life
under the lizard's belly fourteen centuries ago.

To learn Home as the Basketmakers knew it would require the
erasure of modern earthworks—no roads, no contours rearranged
by shovel and blade, as our hillside was, for pasture improvement,
during the antiquities-insensitive forties—and the removal of introduced vegetation—no knapweed, no tamarisk or tumbleweed and
other Eurasian imports. Instead of a ghost floodplain and a channel narrowed by dam control, the river in spring runoff might
fill the valley with sluggish braids that spread a half mile across
but only a few inches deep—no catfish, carp, fathead minnows, or
other nonnative fish; no elevated loads of pesticides and salts.
Drinking the waters of the San Juan might sicken me. The bench
dwellers could die of tooth decay, breach birth, or a broken leg.

A geography common to the Basketmakers and me, without
the thickest filters of imagination, would be stars and rock, the
immutable rock that hones a razor-sharp line between earth and
sky. Science reassures us that the stars shift and the seasons change
without our help. Nevertheless, after the winter solstice I note the
sunrise's incremental motion along the horizon, proof that the
sun's daily arc has indeed lengthened and the year has turned
toward summer. My predecessors also marked the course of the
heavens, with greater vigilance and accuracy, similar anxiety, and
the encouraging dramatic metaphor of prayer and dance.

They chiseled their thoughts on the rock faces along the river
and beyond—bighorn sheep, turkeys, handprints, anthropomorphs
with crooks and headdresses, and all manners of dots, spirals, cir-
cles, and zigzags—and these petroglyphs remain for me to admire

and misinterpret. It is safe to assume that we both stared at the magnificent play of light on the sandstone walls around us, from dawn to dusk and through the seasons an unending source of beauty and exhilaration. Like me, perhaps, they marked the ends of the day by the morning rise of the Canada geese from the river bottom as the birds moved downriver to feed for the day and their noisy, honking return each evening, flying in a low *V* against the red cliffs, their backs and wings as dark as mahogany and their bellies lit to fire with the molten gold of sunset.

For the bench dwellers, much in their environs fell into the categories of menu, magic, and medicine, toolbox, wardrobe, and information. Stones provided pestles, pounders, axes, hammers, and mauls, and walls for pit houses, dwellings with considerable architectural variation but essentially partly subterranean, roundish structures with roofs supported by thick posts. *Manos,* stones shaped to human hands, and grinding slabs, or *metates*, turned corn into meal and a woman's arms into limbs of strength. (The bones of women buried in the midden, for instance, showed well-developed upper-body musculature.) The willows that grew along the river and the squawbushes in nearby canyons rendered pliant fibers for baskets. Yucca plants were used for baskets and nearly everything else, from paintbrushes and hairbrushes to cordage, fishnets, and footwear.

The Basketmaker Anasazi had no wheels, no pockets, no identifiable hats, and no lack of ingenuity. They replaced the atlatl—a throwing stick mounted with a stone-tipped dart, used by earlier hunters—with the bow and arrow. For blankets they wove furry strips of rabbit skin with rows of twine. Mineral-based paints adorned their corded yucca-fiber sandals, some of which had stylish toe loops. They burped, their arms went numb when they slept on them wrong, and they saw their own faces in mirrors of still water. Their pottery was plain gray or painted black on white; their babies were portable. They remembered the past and contemplated their future. They gossiped and dreamed.

Pet dogs moved among them. Domesticated turkeys provided feathers, and eagles suggested great power, evident in the golden eagle skeleton found beneath the floor of one of the pit houses on my bench. With other people in the region, the bench dwellers sought mates and traded information, probably about food, rain, and access to territory should local scarcities require relocation. Trade also brought them shells from the Pacific and Mexico's Gulf of California, mostly *Olivella dama*, a cylindrical shell easily strung on necklaces and bracelets, and *Glycymeris*, a roundish bivalve whose cutout center left an encircling shell edge that was perfect for a bracelet.

Arable land likely attracted these people to this sun-baked valley along the San Juan River. Rain lured from the heavens by ritual, and surface water diverted to fields by flood and check dams, irrigated the farmers' corn, squash, and beans. Then, as now, agriculture localized a diverse food chain, which the bench dwellers fully exploited: cottontails, jackrabbits, various rodents and birds, plus pigweed, amaranth, and other edible weedy annuals that sprouted in soil disturbed by cultivation. (This endows the Saint Thomas Aquinas Cactus and Succulent Society with over fifteen hundred years of weed history.)

The bench had a topographic advantage: it was close to the washes and crops yet protected from floods. Clay provided adobe and, in at least one case, an in situ floor for a pit house. The clay-rich soil horizon of an old coppice dune associated with a greasewood bush had formed one of those rock-hard, nearly impenetrable pans that still, like the greasewood, dot the slope. The builders incorporated this natural, low-maintenance slab into their dwelling.

If there were prehistoric structures on our land, the predam, flood-prone river washed them away or the bulldozers of fifty years ago obliterated them. The nearest intact domicile consisted of two pit houses, a ramada, and storage areas—a sort of prehistoric closet. A catastrophic fire, possibly intentional, burned the place. It was likely abandoned shortly thereafter.

Archaeologists have reconstructed pit houses and set them afire. They have found that a pit house does not burn from a smoking-in-bed sort of carelessness—it is, in fact, surprisingly difficult to burn one—and they have found traces of combustible materials in the ashes, as if plant matter had been used as fuel for a deliberate pyre. Why would these people torch their own homes? Archaeologists hesitate to guess the reason, so they will call it "religion."

Excavation of the pit houses beyond our fence uncovered a rubble of burned posts, beams, and carrizo reeds, which were commonly bound in thick mats and used to line walls. The closet still held, among other things, bundles of human hair (handy for twine and woven leggings), a pouch made from a prairie dog skin, the horn of a bighorn sheep, an unfinished pendant, a burned sandal, and charred flower tops. The Hopi and other Pueblos used this same wild plant, a subspecies of fineleaf hymenopappus, for a ceremonial emetic. They chewed its roots to relieve tooth decay.

I can relate what is known of the Basketmaker burial site, but it is a story told as if in an alien tongue or with a difficult speech problem. Archaeologists carefully decipher the "language" of artifacts, then strain it through their own skill and understanding. Sometimes they end up with a kaleidoscope, other times with a shadow of a shadow. In the sixth-century midden next door to me, bones cast the clearest shadow. The bones tell me how to plot my ancient neighbors on the Map of the Known Universe.

The midden was deep and extensive. It may have collected the castoffs of dispersed villagers for over a century. The human skeletons rested amid the trash—no disrespect intended because everything in the "dump" was headed toward the same destiny: dust. Many bodies lay in close proximity to animal bones, suggesting funerary offerings rather than random fill. If deliberate, the offerings were simple compared with those in other graves of the period, which might load up the departed with food, baskets, dogs, weapons, body ornaments, and a fresh pair of sandals.

The bodies reclined in a flexed position, knees drawn up, arms folded on the pelvis: six men, three women, five children and babies, four fetuses. They wore jewelry and hunger. The youngest was about six months in utero, buried with a small seed jar. The oldest was a man over forty, buried with his earring and eggshells and a Canada goose across his ribs. Nearly everyone, children included, had a shell bracelet on the left wrist. A shroud made from the fibrous bark of a juniper tree wrapped a twenty-year-old, a woman with a notably delicate build. A slightly older woman bore remnants of a burial shroud and signs of malnutrition. Half of a ceramic bowl rested on her shoulder. The other half, near her arm, held the thin bones of heartbreak: a fetus. Had she died in childbirth?

Draped around the torso of one of the interred was a necklace strung with over a thousand *Glycymeris* disk beads, accented with turquoise and olivella shells. One man's skull rested on a stone of yellow oxide, another on a wood fragment underlain with cobbles, those still ubiquitous spheroidal stones polished to near silkiness by the San Juan's ancestral river.

The bones of the bench dwellers tell of human ailments—a

broken clavicle, blows to the head, severe arthritis, infections, poor to nightmarish dental conditions—and anomalies such as spina bifida and bone fusions, the latter in a robust adult with notably developed upper-body musculature, hinting that his infirmities might have made him somewhat sedentary. He was the one with the cobble headrest and an abundance of rabbit, prairie dog, rodent, and other small mammal bones in the burial with him—a decent food supply for a less able hunter, perhaps.

Much of the bone story supports a fairly solid assumption about early desert dwellers: they lived in cycles of plenty and hunger. The hard times could range from seasonal deprivation to periodic starvation. Half of the midden population, children and adults, showed evidence of iron deficiency anemia, which is related to poor diet, infection, and other factors. The bones do not tell everything about my neighbors' lives and deaths, of course—if they drowned or choked on a piñon nut or the squeeze of someone else's hands around their neck. I prefer not to think of them as the dead unfed but as men, women, and children with desert bodies who faced austerity and survived—or did not.

Let us indulge in a fantasy, one of those wildly anachronistic forays into imagination that will elevate our flake status in the minds of dedicated archaeologists and send them lunging for the Valium. Let us presume that the bench dwellers could come forward to the present time for a brief visit. Let us presume that I would hand out dental floss, steel-bladed knives, and many other practical items. I would trade my husband's chain saw for a pair of yucca fiber sandals and one of those nifty, puppy-plump, prairie dog skin pouches. Let us presume that the Valium is taking effect, so we can wallow deeper in fantasy without whining protests from the empiricists.

To settle the "Anasazi" name dilemma once and for all, I would ask the bench dwellers what they called themselves. I would ask them if they had maps. I would ask if descriptions of the ocean passed along the trade network with the olivella shells—how would a person of the slickrock canyons envision *Pacific*? I would show them the time elapse photographs of the Trinity bomb test and try to explain how my century came to its strange pass, where we discovered the invisible quantum world that holds existence together, then promptly devised ways to rip it apart. Silently I would show pictures of Hiroshima and Edvard Munch's painting *The Scream*.

When we open up the discussion, the bench dwellers might squint skeptically at the panorama beyond us and ask, rather testily, "Where the hell is the river?"

Artifacts and faunal remains from the Basketmaker neighborhood speak of a wetter climate and a different San Juan River in prehistoric times, although not radically different from the river of a hundred years ago, before tamarisk invasions and reclamation projects petrified the floodplain. It is likely that the bench dwellers lived beside a lusher riparian ecosystem—more carrizo reeds and other marshland flora, sandhill cranes (a rare visitor these days), the Ross' goose (even scarcer), and an abundance of Canada geese, teals, yellow-headed blackbirds, and other wetland species.

By the time Mark and I came to our land, archaeologists had already excavated the Basketmaker sites on the bench above the old San Juan floodplain. The artifacts were removed to a university museum, and the bones from the burial were made available for reinterment by the Pueblos, the Basketmakers' descendants. Backfill now covers the pit houses and other sites. A highway and its right-of-way obliterate the burial midden. Over it flow BMW sedans, Harleys, and truckloads of grapes, potato chips, floor wax, roof trusses, and the U.S. mail. We live compatibly with the ghosts because there simply are so many.

In a world where much of pre-Columbian "exotica" lies behind museum glass, it may seem strange to live an atlatl's throw from a Basketmaker graveyard. That's how life goes around here—deep history crunches beneath our feet. Despite the valley's remoteness and the bounty of wild country around us, the human overlays are thick, with binding agents as basic as pets and medicine, death and the weather. To the charred flowers and golden eagle bones people gradually add their own strata of cultural debris: Pennzoil bottles, beagles, cheap smut magazines, nuclear fallout, junked Fords. The wind sweeps more sand over the dunes; new grease-wood bushes take hold.

The Basketmaker neighborhood easily fills several folios of the Map of the Known Universe. The "village" and the midden people carry with them to the lizard's belly so many bits of their lives and land. Squash rinds, corncobs, gourd skins. Rabbit bones cast from a meal, the mandible of a fox, blackbird bones as delicate as air. It is the desert that bridges the centuries between us and marks the trails to Home. They knew about consequence, these ancient neighbors on the river terrace. They knew in their bones that a Canada goose buried atop their beloved was quite enough—life, death, sustenance, beauty, all in a single, magnificently wild bird, heavy on a man's chest in a grave beside the river. I would like to think of that goose as *Hisatsinom*, an ancestor of the geese that daily bring me serenity by their mere presence— birds that announce my place, to paraphrase poet Mary Oliver, in the family of things.

Bones of the sandhill crane—a leggy, gray-brown marsh bird with a red crown and a seven-foot wing span—lay in the midden with an adult male and an eighteen-month-old child with an olivella shell bracelet encircling his or her tiny wrist bones. On the Map I sketch a woman in a red velvet bathing suit with an entourage of sandhill cranes. Thinking about a ghost river edged with a teeming spraddle of wetlands, I draw more waterbirds: snowy egrets, herons, ibises, ducks, white pelicans, and others that fill today's river corridor during the ultra-high-water years, when the dams and reservoirs cannot steal everything, and the San Juan tries to spill into its ancient floodplain.

I sketch a poorly generic bird (how do you draw tenderness?) for the unnamed songbird found in the fill near the skeleton of a two-year-old. In the midden the youngest lay near the tallest, an arthritic man about forty years old. This fellow, too, wore a shell bracelet on his left wrist. In the fill with him were squirrel, prairie dog, and black-tailed jackrabbit bones. He also shared his tomb with the remains of another precious little earthling of fatter river times: the slender pelvic bone of an amphibian, genus *Bufo*. He died with a toad.

A map overlays time, place, and journey. It helps us to understand our location. In a single dimension it gives three: where we are, where we have been, and where we might go. The idea of a map is to compose one's geography in a way that makes sense of it. The idea of a map is to keep us from becoming lost.

Long before we reduced all of creation—earthly, celestial, galactic—to a grid, people carried maps in their heads. For many Australian aborigines, ancestral deities had originally sung the world into existence—every rock, plant, creature, and waterhole on a vast and complex continent. To find your way, you followed the songlines, you sang the land. Thus, one's topography was simultaneously story, music, and place. Greenland Eskimos mapped their intricate coastline on small wooden relief maps, which they carried in their pockets and used to find their way in fog. Families of the Chemehuevi Indians, desert nomads along the Gila and lower Colorado Rivers, matched their territory to the territory of a herd of bighorn sheep. The bighorns' range and landmarks were comparatively predictable. Thus, the sheep defined and mapped land "owned" by humans.

Formal maps, wrote essayist Peter Steinhart, arose when people began to speculate "on more than how to get there from here. [Mapmaking] was spurred by philosophical questions. Is the world orderly and good? Is it full of demons and wonders?" Before the great eras of exploration filled the blank spaces, most maps exaggerated the size and importance of home ground at the expense of outlying territory. Self-inflation placed "civilization" at the world's center and monsters, treacherous chasms, ship-grabbing islands, and other perils on the fringes. Human beings lost the attributes of the ethnocentric group in direct proportion to their distance from the center. Inside the circle: Us. Beyond the circle: Them—"savages," darkness, chaos.

I, too, made the Map of the Known Universe a circle, a cosmic diagram of personal experience bound to an intimate geography. It had a center (the ground beneath the lizard's belly), but, like the four sacred peaks that defined the safe world of my Navajo neighbors, I held less strongly to the idea of a center than to concentric spaces that, outside the Map, became progressively more alien.

I had intended a non-European map, an antimap that revealed the red-rock desert through the doors of perception, one that was gloriously indifferent to explanations, to the etiologic glue that held it together. I neither wanted nor needed my precise location. I preferred to be lost. What spurred me were neither philosophical nor practical questions, not Is this place orderly or demonic or griddable? but *Just how beautiful is it?* In my wanderings, in my not-everyday life, at least, I adopted an awkwardly personal version of an Arab's view. The classical Arabian object in life was to Be—free, brave, wise—or just Be, contrary to the rest of the world, whose aim is to Have—knowledge, things, a name.

The true Map of the Known Universe bound ephemeral aesthetics, the subtle and the private, to concrete spaces. It elevated the exquisite tension between stasis and motion, between Home and my innate, incurable restlessness. To rechart my own terrain, I simply had to explore it with reflexes, not reason, with lips on the scarlet velvet of claret cups, bones and skin absorbing every molecule of sand, river, rock, and lucid desert air. All I had to do was savor the desert stillness, that spare landscape of absence and seeming nothingness that in the end I knew to be so potent and full. The Map of the Known Universe, I had hoped, would be a witness of the senses, a map of my own body.

Following a night of wailing violence outside the screenhouse, I sat myself down in a decrepit lawn chair beside a sliver of ditch water and hoped for toads. At first it seemed the proper refuge to still the fermenting ironies that grew yeastier with each foray into the Known Universe. I dragged with me, however, not soporific Thoreau or sinuous Rilke but *The Los Alamos Primer* and a treatise on particle physics that promised once and for all to unravel the cosmic onion.

In the night, under a placid full moon and a lulling chorus of crickets, a pack of coyotes had tried to rip apart one of their mates. The coyotes fought close to the screenhouse, oblivious to our presence or accustomed by this time to thinking of Mark and me as occupying the low end of the "interesting" spectrum, somewhere down a notch from fence posts. The assault seemed to push the night's amorphous velvet to the edge of a knife blade. On and on went the aggressive snarling, the victim clearly yelping in fear and submission until only the assailants could be heard. In the daylight, to the honking clatter of the Canada geese—they, too, sounded fitful and restless—I surveyed the scene of the struggle for far-flung chunks of *Canis latrans,* from which I could read the story of the night's terrible discord.

I found animal parts, but they were not coyote. They were four bits of black-tailed jackrabbit: two hind legs, severed at the hip, and two ears. The legs and ears lay together on the sand in perfect rabbit assembly, as if the creature was in connect-the-dots profile, sitting on its haunches, with air instead of a body between its ears and rump. A few tufts of soft gray hair clung to the nearby rabbitbrush; otherwise no blood, no guts, simply these long, speedy limbs and the slender ears, mapped with scarlet veins now cold and fading. This puzzle was not easily deciphered.

I imagined the moonlit black-tailed jackrabbit, pounced upon and unaware of its doom or flushed out and leaping twenty feet at a time, jumping quite high every few leaps for a better view of its pursuer, then pushing to racing speed as the chase grew serious. A pack is not needed to bring down even a good-sized rabbit buck. One coyote will do. Perhaps other coyotes had joined the killer, then ganged up viciously on an intruder, and what I heard was the noise of a battle over food.

The bunny legs looked so silly there on the ground with their huge hind feet and leathery toe pads. The ears measured at least five inches, silky and tender, brownish with jet-black tips. I stroked them, tried them on my own head. I held them up to the sun to see the scarlet translucence of light that passes through delicate mammal ears.

I abandoned coyotes and hiked along the drainage ditch that ran through a section of our land, where I hoped to determine if the ditch's standing water was hospitable to amphibians. I had neither seen nor heard toads there, yet it was the closest even by a long stretch to what may have once been a slough of wetter times and the old, sprawling river. The sun sat high, not the time of day for toad watching, but a scruffy patch of saltgrass next to the ditch appeared so enticing, I fetched chair, books, and Map and sat down beside the water.

Spring days in the desert begin with a wild shriek of raucous life madly intent on reproducing itself. The afternoon perched on a quieter exhalation of afterglow, plump with warm sun and non-specific hums and drones that seldom fail to induce a drowsy reverie about nature's endless miracles, the fullness of life, and thermonuclear reactions in hydrogen.

In *The Los Alamos Primer*, a collection of lectures describing Manhattan Project bomb physics by Robert Serber, one of the project's theoreticians, Serber mentions a blackboard at the Los Alamos weapons laboratory during a postwar conference on the hydrogen bomb, a device nudged out of the darkness by physicist Edward Teller and nicknamed the Super. Delivery, or how to get this post-Trinity generation of weapons to their targets, initially presented more problems than concept or engineering. The first true thermonuclear explosion, in the South Pacific in 1952, code-named Mike and infamous for vaporizing the entire island of Elugelab (its yield was a thousand times Hiroshima's), began in a refrigerated warehouse, a six-story-high, open-air "shot cab"—not exactly something one could slip tidily into a casing or missile, although the H-bomb quickly became so, multiplying its yield even as it shrank.

At the conference Teller's blackboard listed designs for nuclear weapons by their strengths, properties, and capabilities. For the last weapon on the roster, the largest, Serber recalls that "the method of delivery was listed as 'Backyard.' Since that particular design would kill everyone on earth, there was no use carting it elsewhere."

Most of us deal with the world of appearances through intuition and senses. By nature our minds cannot form an adequate picture of the intricate details that underlie ordinary matter. The laws of physics do this for us; they reconstruct reality in graceful metaphors such as mathematics, with as much beauty as the natural forces they describe. The implicit assumption is that the universe, even the subatomic universe, bears an ultimately knowable symmetry.

For the inquisitive mind, of course, explaining *how* the world works can be as aesthetically rich as understanding, with our senses, that the world *is*. As poet John Donne wrote, the urge to knowledge is the most ungovernable of all the passions. In this light, Backyard on the blackboard had its beauty—the elegant, conceivable "truth" that matter could be made into the fire of a star—but a beauty so dangerous, it was morally inconceivable, even in the inert chalk of an equation.

Under the bright spring sun I wore a headdress of semilethargic flies. Heckle—or Jeckle?—cruised overhead, giving his best turkey imitation. When I pretended not to notice, he flew over again, a perfectly respectable adult raven going *gobblegobblegobble*. The sliver of water lay between shaggy banks of saltgrass, its edges frosted white with dried salts. The insects were there—around my head, amid the lacy fronds of tamarisk, above the shiny surface of the small pool—but no amphibian predators appeared. I wondered if the habitat was too alkali even for alkali-tolerant toads.

At the end of World War II the atomic pioneers in Serber's circle turned much of the work of arsenal enhancement over to the technocrats. The basics were in place; to the how-to and how-big, the cold war added how-many and where-do-you-want-them.

Then, at the close of the cold war, the paradigm shifted once again, from a petroleum-based phallogocentric era of missiles and hardware, as one rather insightful person has suggested, to a cyberspacious, information-based scrotal era, in which discreet, intumescent storage, or big balls, is more important than a big . . . well, you get the picture.

Since the beginning of the century, physicists have been peeling away layers of matter like the layers of an onion, peering deeper into the structure of the subatomic universe, where they find more and more bricks. Nuclei, the pets of the atom splitters, are themselves loci of whizzing particles, which are composed of successively deeper levels of structure best imagined not as solid, fixed *things* but as minuscule, vibrating strings, not as invisible motes but as "tendencies to exist" or "tendencies to happen," an unending dance of interactions. The exploration of subatomic architecture has revealed even more fundamental constituents called quarks, the pets of the particle physicists. There are (so far) six species, or "flavors," of quarks, each flavor a triplet of "colors" and some with "hidden beauty," others with "naked beauty"— that is, characteristics expressed as descriptive idioms.

This hall of mirrors has also revealed more about neutrinos, the pets of the apocalyptists, which are massless ghosts of radioactive decay produced by the sun and other celestial bodies and showered to Earth every second by the billions but so weakly interactive they pass right through everything, including your body. A few scientists speculate that enough neutrinos from a collapsing star might every 100 million years or so bombard us and wipe out a great deal of DNA. One reason we know neutrinos exist is that scientists set up a detection target in the form of a deep mine in South Dakota and filled it with half a million liters of dry-cleaning fluid, which then "picked up" neutrinos in chance chemical interactions.

Quarks may have even tinier parts, many still in the head-scratch-and-mutter stage and yet to be revealed by high-energy accelerators that study the debris of collisions and resolve the sub-atomic realm in finer detail—relatively speaking, of course, since the primary character of elementary units of matter is their intangibility. Over the years particle accelerators have become mammoth circular structures. For a super supercollider, nicknamed the "desertron" and at least thirty miles in diameter, researchers are, in the great physics tradition, seeking a flat piece of dry, nothing-out-there American outback. Imagining what such a machine might discover is called "populating the desert." Perhaps to truly know anything, scientists will have to go still further and build a bagel the size of a galaxy. Whatever it takes, when we do understand the particle zoo, we shall be able to relate, in the birth of the universe, the eensiest nanoquantum to the biggest bang. We shall have cracked one gigantic knowable. We shall have the Theory of Everything, known fondly among the cognoscenti as TOE.

The pool was as still as glass. There might have been a line of drool down my chin. For certain, Heckle—or Jeckle—had passed out. Strung across the page of my book, the intricate strands of numbers and equations looked like squirrel fur.

Ever since the day we lifted our knuckles off the ground, we *Homo sapiens* have sought to explain things. Everyone wants the Meaning of Life, a divine or secular grand design, which is probably not a single thing but the refraction of millions of minds trying to figure it out. I closed the book and pulled out the Map.

From up the hill Mark yelled to me. I remembered that we had planned to do a bit of desert-rat-style *feng shui*, or "perfect placement," to define more precisely the location of our house site on the bench. Our brand of geomancy, a sort of acupuncture of the earth, consisted of driving a few stakes into the dirt and hoping that when the backhoe excavated the foundation, it would not unearth any dead bodies. For the moment, I ignored his call.

Quarks, I thought, were sort of how I was feeling about the Map of the Known Universe. It had acquired a certain *shadowy reality*.

At the onset the idea had been simple: to chart my own terrain. The Map encompassed the two-hundred-square-mile neighborhood around me, an egocentric version of the ancient ethnocentric maps. Inside the circle was familiarity, holiness, passion. Outside, senses dulled, I lost the shark in my own spirit.

The first trek took me to Tsé Valley. Nothing in particular guided me there save an appetite for a cactus and the delectable lure of Tsé k'aan, the ridge of tilted sandstone that sliced through the Known Universe, a seduction that not even the most unadventurous doorknob could resist. In Tsé Valley I found a fossil river, a ghost of what is now the desert's most unlikely glory and most precious gift. Where had those waters led me? Off the circle. The island of Trinity rose up and grabbed me like a passing ship.

Trinity loaded into one morality-charged wallop the desert's strange paradox as the natural terrain of the spirit and the proving grounds of mass death. I studied my sketches from the Jornada del Muerto: pupfish, toads, unrepentant nuggets of plutonium with Tsé Valley's name on them. African oryx and Stealth bombers. An oxymoronic military wilderness that was in some sectors more "pristine," perhaps, than my own national park–stuffed Four Corners home turf. Then I scuttled my glow-in-the-dark butt back under the lizard, mindful that it might be best to know a smaller place and try to earn it—weeds, water, neighbors dead and alive.

Mark called to me again. I wondered if I should find Heckle and resuscitate him. There were no toads near the ditch at the moment and, considering their squat blobbiness, who needed them? On the other hand, how could I lure them back? What if we myth-hungry *Homos* spent less time on heavy leptons and galactic bagels and reservoirs of dry-cleaning fluid and more time on Eden?

One way to reclaim toad habitat would be to dismantle the megadam upstream so that the river in flood sprawled against the bench, as it may have in Ancestral Puebloan times, creating sloughs and ephemeral pools. Not possible without a lengthy prison term. Another method would be a kind of reverse terrarium: provide optimal but somewhat studied conditions and hope they worked in the field.

Sensitive naturalists advise against rearing toads as household inmates. It is better, they say, to start and end with tadpoles, to run a healthy nursery aquarium but release your wards when they become young terrestrials. Part of the problem is the emotional consequence of imprisoning wild creatures in a glass box: the corpuscular acid of miserable, bleeding-ulcer guilt that will rack your entire being forever. Obstacles of a more utilitarian nature include keeping a lid on and feeding the ravenous little buggers. Vegetarians that grow up to be carnivores make obvious gastronomic demands. As their legs form and grow, toads hop around and want meat. They will bash their tiny heads on their glass or screen ceiling. They will tire of cat and dog food. Only in their natural habitat will they find the constant supply of insects that they need.

I thought of the extreme and ascetic environment at Trinity. There the toads survive the harsh Chihuahuan Desert by cheating drought. They burrow beneath the desert, reduce their oxygen consumption, and absorb moisture from the soil through their skin, something few other vertebrates besides amphibians can do. They reduce life to the lowest ebb.

On my moister but not overtly lush chunk of Colorado Plateau, I believed, toad life would require only a setting in which beauty could operate. Much of it was in place: tumbles of smooth river stones with crevices for shade and shelter, glimpses of fine blue sky and sumptuous slickrock, spring air like warm velvet, tiny red-orange jewels of damselflies alighting on the emerald fronds that bordered the small pool. On slightly higher ground could be found abundant red sand in which a bufo or spadefoot might wrap itself, there to lie in a quiet trance until its skin could manage the open air again. In essence, if all was right with that extraordinary toad hide, all was right with the world.

A toad's skin, among the most complex in the animal kingdom, is an organ of perception. To reclaim the Known Universe properly, I had to become an organ of perception. To get back on the Map, I had to pass through the surfaces of things. I had to be a better Arab. I would disregard the particles and listen to the unexplained spaces between them, reclaim the conditions for beauty. If the piranhas of historical circumstance insisted that I decode some dim message about the peculiar marriage between deserts and physics . . . no, it simply weighed too much.

I stashed books and chair and headed back to meet Mark. On my way through the tamarisks I again examined the scene of the coyotes' furious battle. Although the rabbit appendages still offered no clue to the night's violence, the memory of its sounds returned, cries of bloodletting and torn flesh, the anarchy of a pack against the one. Indulgent hedonism, I thought, is an incomplete approach to the Known Universe; nature requires an alertness to antagonism as well as harmony.

The luxuriant spring day thinned the night terrors. The sun

burned the distant sandstone cliffs to fire—crimson, vermilion, and gold on their face, deep indigo in their shadows. The land seemed gloriously vibrant, incapable of resisting so overwhelming an intensity of color. In the sun on my shoulders I felt a hint of the coming summer's ferocious heat.

At the foot of a crumbling cutbank on the property line, I stopped to pound in a fence post that had not been set deep enough into the soft ground. Beyond this edge of the property ran a remnant of an old highway, abandoned twenty years before, and, despite the desert's slow pace of decay, impressively disintegrating and sprouting a brisk crop of weeds along its sunbleached yellow passing stripe. The eroded cutbank below the old tarmac exposed gravel and river cobbles and a few rusty cans and bottles tossed from passing cars when the old road carried its load of desert wayfarers.

Instead of fetching a post pounder, I looked among the stones for a likely substitute. An odd rock drew my eye. It was not smooth and gray like the others but dull, chunky, and yellowish, with a slightly powdery cast and a better grip than the dome-shaped river stones. I dislodged it from the dirt and carried it to the fence post to use it as a pounder.

Oops.

I screamed and let go of the rock as if someone had just handed me Backyard. The rock hit the ground with a terrible thud. It was right there under the lizard's belly.

Hydrous potassium uranium vanadate. Carnotite. The raw ore for yellow cake.

Spitting Photons
Through Vacuums
of Folded Space

On the day I visited Los Alamos, the nuclear weapons laboratory was quite concerned about my breasts.

The lab had a piece of technology that could resolve soft tissue more accurately than state-of-the-art medical imaging, a news item announced. By extending the range of current mammography, the technique would help women detect and treat breast cancer. Publicity or security obscured the device's original purpose—military voyeurism, planetary incineration, whatever. Nor was mention made of how the U.S. Department of Energy facility, which over the past half century helped to arm the nation with thousands upon thousands of packets of supreme death, had gone into the breast business.

Although national defense has always driven the great repository of brain capital at Los Alamos, the lab and other defense research institutes have never hesitated to extend their knowledge and their tools to civilian applications. World War II and the cold war produced a "technological piñata" (John McPhee's words) for virtually every science from medicine to meteorology. The U.S. Department of Defense, in fact, is now second only to the National Cancer Institute in its funding of breast cancer research. Body parts are but one of many beneficiaries on the road to Armageddon.

The Los Alamos National Laboratory stopped making atomic weapons in 1989. Since then it has directed a reduced workforce to dismantle the U.S. nuclear arsenal and help clean up the mess, as well as continue research unrelated to weapons. We taxpaying fund-raisers hold faith in Los Alamos's ability to baby-sit our investment, the remaining stockpile. Taming those outlaw spasms of abject terror with polite albeit imperfect trust, partial nuclear disarmament is now like checking one's firearms at the door of the saloon, all but the little bitty one in your sock.

Today the same industry whose test explosions left traces of "sunshine units," or radionuclides, in human tissue was sharing a weapon against the hazards of petronuclear living. So there we have the arms race in a capsule: fifty years of high-gear building and banging followed by untold years of debuilding and unbanging. Only an unsmelted fruitcake like me, dragging a seven-pound chunk of raw carnotite up the Pajarito Plateau in the back of her truck on a cold, wet day in the high desert, would wonder at the elements of lunacy in human history.

Along the highway between Santa Fe and Los Alamos the New Mexico license plates said "Land of Enchantment," and the flashy marquees on the Indian casinos declared "Loose Slots." A billboard promoted tourism in a one-company town with deep budget cuts, an identity crisis, and its eye on economic diversity: "Explore

Los Alamos: We have enchantment down to a science." The highway crossed the Río Grande and rose up the steep face of the Pajarito Plateau, a shelf of land against the loftier bulk of the Jemez Mountains, then passed through a forest of ponderosa pine and pink and buff cliffs of volcanic tuff.

The retro resort of Los Alamos and its industrial complex sit atop narrow fingers of land separated by deep canyons. From Santa Fe, at night, the lights of Los Alamos appear to hover in a middle world, tenuously affixed to the mountains' ethereal darkness. From Los Alamos itself, the views are magnificent. The laboratory compounds are closely guarded with chain-link fence and razor wire, the mountain air is thin and lucid, and the intellectual stratosphere is thick. When the Manhattan Project scientists set up quarters here in 1943, Hungarian physicist Leo Szilard, whose preferred habitat was a hotel lobby, proclaimed, "Nobody could think straight in a place like that. Everyone who goes there will go crazy."

Now, as then, a considerable number of people in Los Alamos are paid to think. These days, they are more likely to think about vector bosons or nonlinear dynamic systems than about bombs. Some will tell you that the thinkers have dwindled since the early nineties and that the bean counters now outnumber the coneheads. The workforce is highly educated, awash in Ph.D.s who cannot talk publicly about their work. I had yet to spot anyone so absorbed in thought about plasmatronic heat aggression or algorithmic randomness, he or she ran into a lamppost.

The pine-cloaked mesa cried out for a naturalist's study à la White Sands Missile Range—ponderosa, aspen, chokecherry, mule deer, ravens, and the random monkey, beagle, elk, pig, and other species used in radiation studies, then buried in hot dumps set among off-limits compounds known as "tech areas." Atop the mesa and into a compact, pleasantly tidy downtown, one senses that Los Alamos freeze-dried in the early sixties, around the time of the atmospheric-test-ban treaty. The town crossbreeds suburbia with a mountain retreat and university campus run by a technocracy. A lot of sick people have come here.

By this I mean that even before the Manhattan Project, the arid, high-altitude mesa attracted people in need of healing. J. Robert Oppenheimer came from New York to vacation at his family's cabin east of Los Alamos in the early twenties and again, in 1928, to recuperate from an unconfirmed case of tuberculosis. By the time he directed the atomic bomb effort, his attachment to New Mexico was already two decades deep. "My two great loves are physics and desert country," he told a friend years before the Manhattan Project, "it's a pity they can't be combined." Aides to General Leslie Groves recommended that the Army locate its clandestine lab in the townlet of Oak City, Utah, lost in the remote deserts of the Great Basin. Oppenheimer convinced Groves otherwise, and they brought the bomb to New Mexico.

The U.S. Army evicted the mesa's previous tenant, the Los Alamos Ranch School, a place where frail boys grew into robust young men on a diet of classics and rigorous outdoor living. Nearly year-round the boys wore shorts and bedded down on unheated sleeping porches to toughen them up. When a new boy arrived, the school's first task was to undo the work of his mother. Vacuum cleaners had ruined women, the headmaster believed. With nothing to do, mothers spent all their time turning their sons into whimpering doormats.

Ashley Pond, himself "a delicate boy" who took the New Mexico cure, founded the school in 1917 and turned it into a self-contained community with dormitory, stables, a handsome log lodge next to a pond, and a stone shed that during the school's tenure held a year's supply of ice cut from the pond each winter and during the Manhattan Project held the world's supply of plutonium.

And here I was, president-for-life of the Saint Thomas Aquinas Cactus and Succulent Society, parked near the old log lodge and the well-groomed, grassy spaces around Ashley Pond, the pool of water named for the ranch school's founder. Witness to all kinds of frightening activities in the early days, the site is known locally as Ashley Pond Pond and rumored to be hot. I had infiltrated the nation's premier ghetto for the gifted and talented. I had my funny yellow rock.

Parents of baby boomers like me share a communal biography about World War II. Their mantra, "There was a war on—we had to drop the bomb to save lives," resides in context, battle weariness, and a seemingly unchanging world of irrefutable logic. Los Alamos curates its mantra in numbers and heavy metal. At the Bradbury Science Museum the "lifesaving" devices included replicas of the giant steel egg that encased Fat Man (Nagasaki's fire, Trinity's twin) and Little Boy, the "elongated trash can with fins" that destroyed Hiroshima.

I had once visited another of New Mexico's museums of the atomic age, one I called Boner Park for its outdoor garden of inert, lifesaving rockets and missiles—slim, pointed, erect, and aimed roughly in the direction of Texas. The museum's informational film dated to 1963 and never mentioned Nagasaki. An interactive, touch-screen exhibit describing the government's high-level radio-active waste disposal program was out of order. The gift shop sold tiny chocolates shaped like the Fat Man and Little Boy bombs.

The Bradbury Museum was far more sophisticated. Care had

been taken to combine cool objectivity with technology's vertiginous spectacle. One exhibit explained laser fusion. Another examined DNA. Los Alamos, I presumed, had placed itself squarely on the twenty-first century's ground zero, the human gene.

More seductively scary were the contents of a smaller room in the Bradbury Museum and in the nearby Los Alamos Historical Museum: household items, ordinary artifacts, the myths of Los Alamos told in security passes for six-year-olds, film badges to measure radiation exposure, and sheet music for a "Vict'ry Polka."

During the life span of the Manhattan Project, this was Los Alamos's known universe: a fence enclosing the town, guarded by military police. A population that by 1945 numbered over eight thousand, average age 29.4 among the scientific staff, most likely faculty or graduate students raided from universities. Intelligence files on the whole lot of them, noting anyone with an "interest in jazz" as suspect. Nicknames for one another: the longhairs (scientists), the plumbers (engineers), the creeps (military intelligence agents). Office janitors hired from nearby Indian pueblos (and hill folk hired at Los Alamos's sister facility in Oak Ridge, Tennessee) because they posed no security threat: to empty trash cans, which often contained discarded notes and memos, you had to be illiterate.

Los Alamos had the inventor of the cyclotron, a South Dakotan who loved to roller-skate. Weekend square dances called by a butcher and an Italian Nobel laureate who danced to them only after he had figured out the steps mathematically. A spy for the Soviets, a painfully shy German emigré whose physics and waltz were flawless. A colony of British scientists who thought Los Alamos was Typical American Life. Twenty-six fatalities in four years, most by construction and traffic accidents; more than one death by falling, radiation exposure, self-administered poison, accidental ingestion of ethylene glycol, and accidental shooting; one drowning and one death by "smudge-pot explosion."

Wartime Los Alamos had mud, diaper shortages, censored mail, rumors of prostitutes, cheap rents, and the Harvard University cyclotron. Brownies, Scouts, French classes, a town council, two dance bands, and a weekly colloquium on physics. A radio station with no call letters, a soda fountain, and a ski hill. A Baudrillardian dream of a trailer park—"hutments" and Quonsets and flimsy boxes hastily assembled to accommodate an urgent mission and booming population.

This is what Los Alamos had: churches, schools, a theater, a symphony orchestra, teas, cocktail parties, alcoholics, and a mystique—in the words of physicist Freeman Dyson, "a brilliant group of city slickers suddenly dumped into the remotest corner of the Wild West and having the time of their lives building bombs." Los Alamos had punch served in chemical reagent jars and seven thousand fire extinguishers. It had no unemployment, no jail, no parking tickets, and no in-laws.

This is what I had after staring at the museum's Kodachrome gallery of mushroom-cloud wargasms over Nevada and the South Pacific: a nosebleed.

The photographs of the bomb tests shared a small room with artifacts from prehistoric Indian ruins on the mesa, trinitite under a box of glass, Oppenheimer's office chair, a melted windowpane from Nagasaki, and a nineteenth-century Bohemian perfume bottle tinted with uranium to the same yellow as my rock. Neither large nor heavy, the bomb pictures hung in parlorlike proportions to the perfume bottle, a background decor of gaudy blossoms or a portrait gallery of household pets.

The bombs erupted thunderheads of incendiary reds and chilling blues, some on squat, thick columns, others ethereal nimbuses on slender stems, each bomb a tiny sun. Charlie, Fox, King, Mike the first thermonuclear, the 10.4-megaton island vaporizer that, like the bikini swimsuit inspired by the atoll of the same name, blew everything away. Hornet, Romeo, Seminole, Oak, Sunset. All of this was happening in Nevada while I listened to *Winnie the Pooh* in my flannel pajamas with little ducks on them. Truckee, Chama, Starfish Prime, Bluestone, and Bravo, each with a heart mined from the Tsé Valley and other fossil rivers on the Colorado Plateau.

They cannot fit them all on the wall. Scorpion, delayed for a day because of a rat in a pipe. Puny Plutonium bomb, the "P.P. Shot" and first dud. The series of series that included "clean" tests (scant radioactive fallout) and tests deliberately made "dirty," usually by adding a cobalt wrap. Tumbler-Snapper, Plumbbob, Teapot, and Upshot-Knothole, a particularly dirty series of eleven detonations that showered rural Utah "Downwinders" with deadly radio-activity and created what some consider an epidemic of cancer and childhood leukemia. The Castle series with its Runts ("weapon-ized Mikes"), and Buster-Jangle, whose ground zero became a test garden for radishes.

As I traded duck pajamas for wool kilts and knee socks, the Doorstep series "translated" the mannequin families near ground zero in Doom Town, Nevada. The smallest bombs were "kittens." A portable nuclear reactor in Antarctica was Nukey Poo. The atomic ejaculations for Dr. Freud: Sugar, Nectar, Climax. All of the bombs were powerful. Most of them were cheap. For Freeman Dyson, who warned his cold war colleagues against nuclear weap-ons as a romantic adventure, cheapness was the bomb's "peculiar horror." He estimated that the cost of adding another Hiroshima, or twenty kilotons, to the destructive power of the hydrogen bomb was about ten bucks in 1950 dollars. "I have felt it myself, the glitter of nuclear weapons," he told an interviewer in the film *The Day After Trinity*. "It is irresistible if you come to them as a scientist . . . to feel it's there in your hands to release this energy that fuels the stars, to let it do your bidding and perform these miracles that lift a million tons of rock into the sky."

No one else in the museum was clawing her way across the carpet, shrieking. The other visitors examined a model of the Cray computer or stood beside the unarmed bomb casings, quietly stroking the steel.

A teacher guided his elementary school class through the exhibits. The girls took notes. The boys did not.

"Where do they keep all the bomb guts?" one boy asked about the Fat Man casing.

"What's over there?" another inquired of an adjacent room.

"More bombs," the teacher replied, "just more bombs." His voice cast a faint trace of android fatigue induced by too much time spent among the terminally precocious. *One more question and I'll stick your little pinhead into that box of trinitite.* A deep reservoir of patience revived him, unimpeachable against the children's innocent faith.

"Just more bombs," he repeated quietly, steering his covey of fifth graders toward the door. "Time for lunch."

Comments in the museum's Public Forum Notebook sighed in relief over the end of the arms race and acknowledged the noble infamy paradox. "I think this is a good museum and you should stay here but I think bombs suck," one visitor wrote. Lest anyone forget the ideological chasm between Los Alamos and Santa Fe, geographically intimate kingdoms of physics and New Age metaphysics, someone troubled by Los Alamos's impaired karma left a business card promoting therapy sessions on "synchronicity, nonlocality, and quantum near-death experiences." Written across the top of the notebook page in block letters was a single word: AGGRESSION.

I hauled my sunshine units out of the museum's Great Hall of Euphemisms and into a nearby book and gift shop, armed with the name of an outfit that I hoped would shed some light on my yellow rock. I asked the clerk to direct me to the Los Alamos Sales Company. She had a keen eye for the world's bottom feeders, one of which had apparently just slogged out of the shallow end of the gene pool and washed up into her corner of Nerdville, New Mexico. Perhaps she had spotted the carpet fibers hanging from my fingernails.

"Do you mean the Black Hole?" she asked.

I mumbled something about a place that bought and sold surplus goods from the laboratory. Some of the karmic goo from Santa Fe had trickled up the mesa to this shop: angel books, herbal essences, crystals, Kokopelli pencils, bright pink-and-turquoise carvings of coyotes as plump as collies, wearing Texas barbecue bandannas around their necks and throwing their heads back in totemic New West howls. I wondered if I should mention the carnage in my tamarisk thicket. I decided to buy a couple of pencils.

Rather quickly the woman's wariness evolved into sincere concern—surprising, I thought, for someone too young to have ducked-and-covered under her school desk.

"Are you sure you want to go to the Black Hole? You want to talk to Ed?"

"Who is Ed?" I asked.

"Ed Grothus. He owns the Los Alamos Sales Company—the Black Hole," she explained. "Are you alone? Do you plan to go there by yourself?"

Oh how festive, I thought, I just happen to be seeking Los

Alamos's one and only black-market beagle dealer. However, I had not come all the way from Utah with my stupid blob of yellow cake, a Manichaean burden, and a heart-wrenching lapse of faith in all humankind only to be leered at by some unbuttoned oyster with a thing for pinto dogs or chains and metal, even if they were federally subsidized chains and metal. With an it's-your-funeral flick of her pen, the young woman drew me a street map to the Black Hole.

"Is this Ed some kind of pervert?" I ventured. What could be worse in this hamlet of denial? Homeless people? Brie vendors? Democrats? She gave me another pensive frown.

"Oh no, he's a gentleman. He . . ." She paused, then blurted it out. "He writes letters. To the editor."

The Kokopelli pencils rested in my fingers, reeking their virginal yellow pencilness. The nebulous malaise of soul, provoked by the boiled lizard, suddenly leaped into an extremely advanced stage. I felt the reverse of the phantom limb syndrome, an overwhelming body density, as if I were ankle-cuffed to commercial laundromat appliances. When I closed my eyes, the Upshot-Knothole series burned mushrooms into my retinas. *Life is a harrowing event.* My shoulders slumped wearily. *I honestly don't feel like paying.*

Somehow I pulled money from my wallet and paid for the pencils. I asked, "Is the Black Hole safe? Is it radioactive?"

"No," she replied to my second question. "Ed just collects surplus hardware from the lab, mostly scrap and obsolete instruments. You couldn't build a, you know, a device, from his stuff."

Her frown deepened. Then she leaned closer, ready to blister into my brain the horrific, naked truth. She handed me the map and gave me a stern look.

"He's a communist."

•   •   •

Apparently children younger than my fellow baby boomers spent nights lying awake in terror of The Communists, the formless boogie persons of the fifties and sixties who waited in force to pluck American children out from under their Roy Rogers sheets. I slept through it, I guess. A far more immediate and formidable enemy presented itself in the form of my older brother, who, in a manner typical of a firstborn, was forever trying to get rid of me so he could be an only child. (Once I was out of the picture, he would start working on our two younger brothers.)

Our father, a pilot, worked in the federal aviation bureaucracy. Like the private aeronautics industry it regulated, his agency boomed during the postwar years and generated the prosperity that fed and educated my brothers and me. No matter how vehemently we claimed to have been raised by wolves, the truth remained hard-set: the cold war sponsored comfortable childhoods that would have made us at ease among the families of Los Alamos, who also placed a high premium on the intellectual promise of their children.

We crouched under our school desks, inhaling fumes from linoleum cleaner as the air-raid sirens screeched. We read civil defense manuals that told us not to "wander aimlessly about in large numbers" after a nuclear attack but to stay in shelters until the all-clear sounded and we could resume Normal Life in about nine days, precisely the number of postattack menus our mother could order from the local extension agent and store in our basement. We could help her fill out the change-of-address cards the post office promised to issue to survivors. Lest he be distracted, we could remind our father that the Internal Revenue Service claimed it could resume tax collection and the pursuit of delinquent accounts within thirty days after the Russkies nuked us.

We heard "Hiroshima" so far at the edges of adult conversation, the hundreds of thousands dead could have been white mice. We read our Miss Molecule and Our Friend the Atom comic books. We grew up to be liberal arts majors. For a lifetime—an eternity—we lived in the shadow of the bomb, obedient children of Doom Town, ready for the flash. We did not, however, fear the communists. After all, the communists came to our house for dinner.

The occasion was the visit of a delegation of Russian aviators to the United States, hosted by my father's office, and some diplomat's idea to include a family night on their itinerary. We will give them a Typical American Meal, my mother told us on that hot summer night, and you will be Typical American Children.

The communists brought gifts. I do not recall what my parents received—all four volumes of *Great Ukrainian Generals* or commemorative songbooks from the hacksaw factory unions—but I do remember that my brothers and I were given silver pins shaped like wings, inscribed with the name Aerofløt, the Soviet airline, which we affixed to our plaid J.C. Penney clothes. A hard glare from my mother squelched any thought of mentioning the stacks of airline pins—TWA, Pan Am, Lufthansa, and others garnered on my father's frequent travels—that lay stuffed in our drawers amid the dust balls. My brothers and I, of course, had hoped for head-swallowing, spiky fur hats made from Siberian fox pelts, their front flaps adorned with bold red stars.

None of the Russians spoke English. At dinner the interpreter, a gaunt, pale man who told us he had an ulcer, worked maniacally to translate my mother's description of a Peter Sellers movie. Peter Sellers was like another favorite, Monty Python: you laugh like crazy when you think of them but you had to have been there, so everyone was laughing except the Russians. The interpreter mopped his brow with a rumpled handkerchief and stared down at his plate as if it was heaped with flaming roofing nails and he was expected to eat them. For different reasons I felt the same way. We were having home-baked ham. I hated ham. I hated ham enough to give away state secrets, if I only knew what they were. In her pearls and coppery red hair my mother sat at the table looking like glamorous Brenda Starr of the comic strip—feeding communists, fighting the cold war with her beauty and grace, poisoning her only daughter.

After we were excused from the table, my older brother walked down the hall. He ducked quickly into a closet. As I passed he yanked me inside, then rolled the sliding door shut. Instinct told me that this was not one of his frequent homicide attempts but rare unity under duress. We flattened our bodies against the wall. In the near darkness I could barely make out the faint gleam of our Aerofløt pins. My brother checked them for tiny microphones. "Which one do you think is KGB?" he whispered. We agreed it was the short, stocky man with the buzz haircut, furry hands, and a bulky serf suit woven from furnace lint.

Later in the afternoon this man joined me outside on my swings, without the interpreter, his heavy jacket finally shed in the oppressive heat, his flushed, sweaty face giving meaning to the word *pinko*, which I had heard applied to his countrymen. As we glided back and forth on the swings, he gave an impassioned monologue about the virtues of Leninism (I guessed), his daughter (he showed me her photograph), and his family so far away, all the while chain-smoking weird Russian cigarettes: three-inch-long, hollow white cardboard tubes with an inch of what appeared to be yak dung in their tips. He held the cigarette between his index finger and thumb, palm toward his face.

When the Berlin Wall fell and the Iron Curtain parted, the

communists suddenly had faces, and they were largely those of the hot and tired apparatchik on the swings. Meanwhile, one of their comrades had apparently spent the cold war atop New Mexico's secret mesa, its foremost fly in the ointment.

The Los Alamos Sales Company, also called "The Black Hole— An Unusual Place," with "the world's most diversified stock of scientific equipment," occupied an old Shop 'n' Cart supermarket and an A-frame church that once housed Lutherans but now overflowed with "fallout." From these buildings, glaciers of scrap metal, cable, tubes, pipes, and other junk inched toward the parking lot, calving icebergs of a cannibalized solar energy system rumored to have been scrapped during the Reagan era's lovefest with Big Oil. Although I cannot say what the Lutherans were up to when the church was active, its vintage suggested preachers in aqua leisure suits and sideburns, playing guitars and asking everyone in the congregation to hug the person in the pew behind them. Now the building held neutron absorbers, stacks of instrument modules, voltmeters, multichannel analyzers, a morgue of adding machines, and other industrial effluvia.

A chilly drizzle fell outside into the pines and inside the unheated supermarket onto stacks of metal lockers. The roof leaked in a number of places. The communist, who was not a communist at all but a kindly septuagenarian in an insulated snowmobiler's jumpsuit, introduced himself. As Los Alamos's premier loose electron, as its most publicly vociferous and possibly its only antinuclear activist, Ed Grothus appeared delighted to fill yet another ear with his views.

One of the first things to know about Los Alamos: few who live here care to talk about the moral questions inherent in nuclear weapons work. The second point to remember: the only thing outsiders ever want to talk to locals about are the moral questions inherent in nuclear weapons work. Thus, in a close-lipped, conformist community, this noisy, anomalous "peace heretic" attracted attention. Also, where else but in this midden heap of Big Science could taxpayers sample our purchases for the past five decades?

Before he retired to salvage work and private business, Ed Grothus spent twenty years as a machinist in a lab weapons group. "I loved my work," he told me with a wry grin. "There was no better place to live than Los Alamos during those peacekeeping years when we lived by a policy of 'the more bombs we have, the more we don't use them.' "

The Vietnam War changed him from a bomb maker to the town's archpeacenik, whose oft-cited credo, "One bomb is too many," punctuated an indefatigable one-man crusade to remind Los Alamos of its collective guilt in unleashing the nuclear age. Today in the Black Hole he combined the eccentric passion of a junkophile with the zeal of a missionary. At other times he apologized to Hiroshima on behalf of the United States and wrote letters to the local newspaper. In general the people of Los Alamos either ignored him or wished they could run him out of New Mexico on a rail.

We began the Black Hole tour beside a cartoon that showed a clean-cut fellow in a plaid flannel shirt standing on a street corner, holding a sign that said, "Will build nuclear weapons for food." The cartoon, plus three avocado pits on a cluttered desk and an orange cat the size of a fur-covered Fiat, were the first, last, and only items in the midden heap that I understood.

Cramming aisle after aisle was a dusty jumble of thermocouples, resistors, transistors, vaporizers, liquefied gas dewars, glass piping and beakers, a tower of red, blue, and gray IBM Selectric typewriters, and hundreds of instruments whose names began with the prefix *strobo* or ended with the suffix *meter*. The shelves held digital analyzers, shadowgraphs, attenuators, pneumatic pump control units, and other apparatus that had banged, boiled, boomed, zapped, gurgled, shrunk, cooked, cooled, clunked, crunched, calibrated, computed, audited, X-rayed, welded, melted, and smelted their way through the cold war. The cost of a year's worth of typewriter ribbons might have taught a Puebloan or Tennesseean to read.

"Is the Harvard cyclotron buried in here somewhere?" I asked Ed as we wandered past five-beam oscilloscopes and three-foottall liquid nitrogen thermoses. He shook his head. The cat slunk across a stack of what looked like those outhouse-sized, walk-in stereo components favored by people who took LSD in the sixties.

"What's the weirdest piece of junk in this building?" I wondered.

"I can't say," Ed replied, "not until a certain someone dies. Something came through salvage that I can't talk about yet."

This mysterious quarklet of information was such a magnet for me, I was surprised that half the metal in the Black Hole did not suddenly fly across the room and stick to me. However, Ed spoke no further on the subject.

Somewhere amid the amputated remains of a plasma arc cutter, I suddenly felt the same ache for the Utah desert, the same deep longing for home that had so overcome me at Trinity as I stood on the contradictory terrain of serenity and nihilism. Nothing here but the cat invited touching. The great abstraction of nature—physics and the tools that enabled it—lay across a gnawing chasm from our most tangible experience of nature: the land. Yet here again, on this grand mesa, the two had coupled intimately.

Contrary to Szilard's prediction, no one went crazy here. Then, as now, a collective mission fed the mind; the magnificent high desert nourished body and spirit. Not far beneath our consciousness every one of us wants to fit a piece of the earth to a deeply rooted feeling about the work to be done there. If the Trinity site was ultimately utilitarian, its hard clarity and seeming indifference suited to the work of a test, then Los Alamos, chosen by an instinct of passion, bore a far deeper sense of place.

In their collection of the Oppenheimer letters, editors Alice Kimball Smith and Charles Weiner wrote of the dramatic link between the fruit of the Manhattan Project and its natal landscape: "Oppenheimer saw his new colleagues . . . succumb to the spell of his beloved New Mexico. In time some found the arid beauty of the landscape a stimulant, not a distraction, and claimed they would never have worked so hard and effectively in any other environment."

I could not walk deeper into the Black Hole. I panicked whenever the windows, framing a silver light and a blue-black thickness of pines, left my sight. The dim, drippy supermarket was stuffed to the rafters with what could have been, in a science fiction nightmare, Earth's central brain. Perhaps this entire place *was* Earth's central brain, the ultimate console, its exposed and unkempt innards ticking and lurching clumsily onward, dragging the human race through some outlaw robo-agenda.

A mountainous linguine of insulated cables blocked the window light. Why, oh why, I moaned, was I taking the entire nuclear age personally? Why not stick to my claret cup cacti, gibbous moons, slickrock eroticism, and dead bunny ears? I could never fit this midden heap into the Map of the Known Universe. I managed to scrawl one shaky note: "Big cat. The Racal-Vadic VA3434." Then I felt the imminent onset of another existential nosebleed and bolted for the exit.

Quantum mechanics studies the motion of things that come in small bundles. The fundamental bundle of ordinary light, the photon, streams upon us in floods, and as I say this my skull creaks with a brain straining to wed *photon* to visual imagery—jittery cosmic ripples, luminous ovoid pebbles, sleek dolphins with stars on their noses, arcing through ethereal lagoons of silver-and-blue air—fantasies that aptly explain why in seventh grade, mentally crippled by algebra, I was invited to spend most of my school days in the library or in the art room with blank sheets of paper and pots of bright paint.

My physics book organizes atomic architecture into two categories: bricks (structure) and mortar (forces). The bricks include protons, neutrons, and other particles inside the nucleus and, bumblebeeing out there in atomic suburbia, the electron, carrying its charge in orbit, alert for opportunities to bond with neighbors. The mortar that holds the bricks together also can be quantified, first as a force (nature presents four of them) and then as the particle exchange that mediates, or transmits, the force.

We shall leave the particle physicists to nose around in what they have named weak and strong forces, the mortar at the nuclear level. They like it there, where they found quarks and thought they would stop looking but haven't. Meanwhile, fully aware that the more one understands, the more unfathomable things become, the rest of us wallow in the realm of forces so ordinary, we rarely look at them closely. We feel and perceive them as electromagnetism and as gravity, as static cling and the bowling ball dropped from the Tower of Pisa.

Mediating particles have been identified for all forces except gravity. Experiments that verify their existence do so as the equivalent of scientific explanations for ghosts. You cannot *see* a gluon, walk up to your local Nobel laureate, and ask her to whip one out and pin it to a slab of corkboard. Except for dodging the occasional falling bowling ball, we humans generally preoccupy ourselves with a small part of the event called light. Blessed with complex optical organs, we hover around the narrowest band of the least ghostly of the electromagnetic forces: the visible light spectrum, home of the photon packets. Our eyes are the great photon detectors. When we see colors, we are seeing photons vibrating at different rates. We feel photons as radiant energy, the warmth of sunlight on our skin.

Photons ensnare me at my present location on the Map of the Known Universe. I would like to concentrate on this eternal trembling at the heart of matter, the oscillating disquiet of all things, but at the moment I am the victim of another physics experiment. It involves radiant energy in the form of heat. It is simple and it is painful. I am demonstrating the elementary concept of heat transfer, the exchange of agitated molecules from one object to another. In this demonstration the hot object is raised letters on a bronze plaque atop a concrete monument the size and shape of a tombstone. The heated object is my butt.

Mind awash in the visible light spectrum—the striking emerald band of grassland and pines against the azure New Mexico sky—I failed to think before I sat down on the monument. Heated to near scalding by the afternoon sun, the plaque attempted to singe its likeness through my shorts and across the tender flesh of my derrière like a branding iron:

A 29-kiloton nuclear explosive

Reverse the lettered imprint and add the rest of the sentence:

> A 29-kiloton nuclear explosive was detonated at a depth of 4,227 feet below this surface location on December 10, 1967.

I am on ground zero. Again. I have my chunk of yellow cake and a shovel. I am looking for sheep.

In the Four Corners region southwestern Colorado's San Juan and La Plata Mountains spill a broad skirt of high plateaus across the border into New Mexico. The skirt rumples into broken mesas and basins and rugged canyons that drain into the San Juan River, the upstream stretch of my home river, beyond what I once considered the easternmost extremity of the Known Universe. The presence of the tombstone, however, stitches to the Map a table-land that crests in pine forests lobed with open grasslands. To a slickrock crustacean like me, this moister, tree-rich place, not to mention the underground nuclear test site on top of which I sit, induces a by-now-familiar discomfort, the sense of being home but recognizing nothing.

On this high mesa that is a national forest, one might expect to see gorp-fattened backpackers marching up switchbacks or Boy Scouts building character and bonfires big enough for a funeral suttee or itinerant retirees lounging on moats of astroturf at their camper steps. The main event here is not recreation but natural gas. People generally come in fleets of white pickups as day-users, and they are likely to be "pumpers," the roving field employees of energy companies.

The forest straddles the northeastern flank of the San Juan Basin gas field, a vast reservoir of hydrocarbons locked in sedimentary sandstones. Nearly a hundred miles across the basin, strip mines feed coal to power plants with plumes visible from outer space. Over the ridge beyond me lies water to slake the industrial thirsts: the San Juan River backed up behind Navajo Dam. Plug in your body-piercing devices in Los Angeles, steam your couscous over a low flame in Phoenix, and you will be consuming dead organic matter from Mesozoic and Paleozoic New Mexico.

On my drive to the monument I passed one coyote, a random Apache (the Jicarilla Reservation borders the national forest), and several thousand gasworks units. No vista in any direction lacked a drill site. Dense clusters of pipe and steel rose from pads of cleared earth. Doglegs—the junction of an emerging underground pipeline with a capped riser—dotted the main road every half mile and spur roads nearly as frequently. Valves at the doglegs routed and rerouted gas flow along endless miles of pipeline. Peel back northwestern New Mexico's shag rug of jumbled rock and desert scrub, and you will find a factory of pipes and perforations.

Aboveground, on the pastoral illusion around the monument, piñon, ponderosa, and sagebrush edge up against this patch of open grassland. The meadow rolls gently—no gaping crater here, into which you could dump a few Egyptian pyramids, just sun-drenched grasses and wildflowers blooming a kaleidoscope of summer colors: blue-violet lupine, snowy-white yarrow, yellow snakeweed, purple aster, and globemallow capped with coral heads.

At the meadow's perimeter, near the dirt road where I parked, a painted Forest Service sign explains this site as a point of interest. The rare visitor who stops might read the sign and move on, all terrors so very thoughtfully soothed by the words "The Atomic Energy Commission currently monitors water resources in the surrounding area for radioactive traces." The visitor who walks deeper into the clearing may or may not be overcome by unhappily paranoid thoughts, such as, the AEC no longer exists, what precisely does *currently* mean, and what do the tests reveal? He or she may or may not notice that one side of the monument has been altered. On this face—you must part the grass to find it—rectangles of iron-hard epoxy outline two empty spaces. Whatever was affixed to the block (warning signs? memos of protest?) is there no longer.

Little else in this open flat tells you about the event of 1967 or its subterranean nuclear bubble. No fence. No yellow-and-black trefoil. Just this obscure foot-high marker that nearly branded me. It is a tombstone, to be sure, but one that will slowly, slowly, open a forbidding grave only if someone utters the words.

·   ·   ·

From mercifully deep in the annals of southwestern history comes the story of an Arizona scientist who, a few years after World War II, replicated the earliest experiments in the artificial transmutation of the atom. He achieved fission in *frijolium*, a new element synthesized from Mexican legumes. He split the bean atom.

In its time the frijolium satire underscored a postwar change in attitude about the bomb from anxiety to cathartic optimism, from the stark horrors of Hiroshima and bleak psychic landscapes of annihilation to exalted prophecies of the "peaceful atom." Civilian applications of atomic energy, the visionaries promised, would transform American lives with airplanes and cars driven by tiny chain reactions in tiny nuclear reactors. Controlled fission would power rocket ships to outer space; it would melt snow before it reached the ground. Cheap pellets of U-235 would fire up my mother's kitchen appliances, doing all her work for her like little bugs.

With the atom we would farm bigger and eat better. A 1958 edition of *National Geographic* compared color photographs of moldy oranges and madly sprouting potatoes with two-month-old bread and hot dogs looking "as fresh as ever" because gamma rays had destroyed the microorganisms of decay. Rats ate irradiated food, the author claimed, without harmful effect. "Later, military volunteers tried samples. Congressmen have eaten entire gamma-sterilized dinners." Well, no wonder the cold war dragged on and on.

The bright dreams of an atomic middle class waned as the AEC's mendacious there-is-no-danger mantra failed to alleviate fears about radioactivity, and public outcry successfully diverted Congress's attention from nuked wienies to a ban on atmospheric tests. (Such cycles of apathy and activism, speculates historian Paul Boyer, of numbing-dumbing followed by an increased leverage of fear and protest, may forever characterize the cultural weather of nuclear weapons.) The deep-frozen Cold Warriors, of course, remained deliriously busy with underground tests—unstoppable, a cynic might conjecture, unless studies of health risks shifted from women's breasts to the effects of radiation on male virility, sending the boys tripping over themselves to get to the arms control talks.

As the peacetime applications of the atom shifted away from cars and cake mixers, the technocrats spent a number of years (1957 to 1973) and taxpayers' millions on Operation Plowshare, a bizarre series of experiments in geographic engineering and the pet program of physicist Edward Teller. Plowshare's goal was to "tidy up the awkward parts of the world"—obtrusive mountain ranges, unirrigated Saharas, impassable isthmuses, and other pesky inconveniences of nature—with nuclear dynamite. Plowshare, from the biblical prophecy in Isaiah in which nations turn from war and "beat their swords into plowshares," used contained and cratering explosions to determine the bomb's potential for excavating canals, harbors, and highway rights-of-way, unbending rivers to sewer-line straightness, retrieving natural resources, carving underground chasms for waste or water storage, or, if anyone had suggested it seriously, blowing the ice caps off Antarctica. The Soviet Union, too, lauded the promise of nuclear dynamite in its program, nicknamed (of course) Plowshareski.

From its beginning Operation Plowshare garnered little support. To economists it was a joke; it frayed the public's trust in things nuclear. Surprisingly, the strongest opposition came from Teller's own colleagues, who, by studying the possible side effects of nuclear dynamite, launched the precursor of what became known as the environmental impact statement. Their findings questioned plans to use an atomic device to excavate a harbor in the fragile arctic ecology of Point Hope, Alaska, in 1961. A similar environmental study chilled Teller's proposal to cut a new canal across the Isthmus of Panama with up to four hundred bombs. Nevertheless, Plowshare plowed on.

All but a few of the Plowshare experiments found their proving grounds on western deserts. The national science labs at Los Alamos and at Livermore, California, assembled the devices; they were likely fueled with alien pebbles from Tsé Valley and other Colorado Plateau mines. Beneath this meadow in Apache country, one of Plowshare's atomic bombs rearranged the Known Universe.

In 1961, Gnome, the first in the Plowshare series, popped its 3-kiloton payload a thousand feet underground to see how a nuclear technique behaved in a salt formation. Gnome leaked radioactive steam, which might affect your plans to visit its tombstone amid the mesquite near Carlsbad, New Mexico, a tombstone with an epitaph: THIS SITE SHALL REMAIN DANGEROUS FOR 24,000 YEARS. Shoal, in 1963, quadrupled the punch near Fallon, Nevada. The bulk of Plowshare's cratering work—experiments in canal digging and other excavations—took place at the AEC's Nevada Test Site north of Las Vegas. In all, twenty-six tests formed the core of the Plowshare program.

On the Colorado Plateau, Plowshare recruited the bomb for natural gas production and the extraction of oil from shale. Detonated in 1967 beneath my feet, Project Gasbuggy was the first shot, a joint venture by the AEC, U.S. Bureau of Mines, and the El Paso Natural Gas Company. Government and industry teamed up again for two nuclear detonations in western Colorado: Project Rulison in the Grand Valley between Glenwood Springs and

Grand Junction (40 kilotons, 1969) and Rio Blanco near Rifle (26 kilotons, 1973).

Even in the West's largest energy fields, conventional means could not recover "tight reservoir" gas from sedimentary rock of low permeability and still make a profit. For a time drillers shot the tight sands with nitroglycerin, a technique eventually replaced by hydraulic fracturing with diesel oil then sand and water. At the Gasbuggy site the engineers believed they could use nuclear dynamite to tease the gas from the rock. The method simplified: Blow an enormous chimney in the sandstone, into which the gas will flow from the fractured rock around it. Purify the gas of radioactivity (technique to be determined). Pump away.

The Gasbuggy test successfully increased gas flow when compared to conventional wells, and it also produced unexpectedly high levels of tritium. If marketed, the gas itself would have been radioactive and not exactly welcome through the heater vents and ovens of western homes. The next experiment, Project Rulison near Grand Junction, reduced the tritium and proved that profitable recovery of natural gas would, like the Panama Canal proposal, require multiple explosions in situ. In 1973, the Rio Blanco test generated little gas and a great deal of controversy, especially about groundwater. The criterion for locating the explosions was the presence of natural gas, not the ability of rock formations to hold nests of toxic waste for long periods without contaminating the Colorado River and other water supplies.

As long as nuclear testing took place in Nevada, the "there's nothing out there" state, public concern had remained steady but low-key. However, Plowshare's shots in the Four Corners placed the bomb in the backyard. Opposition escalated locally and found support from politicians and the budding environmental movement. Soon after Rio Blanco, Operation Plowshare collapsed. It was not revolutionary as expected but economically disastrous, environmentally hazardous, poisoned by its association with weapons, and an obstacle to disarmament talks.

During Gasbuggy a miniature industrial compound covered the meadow in northwestern New Mexico. Only a few relics remain, among them a culvert sunk several feet into the ground and covered with an openwork metal grille. The shallow pit contains a steel wellhead, capped and slightly rusty at its edges, a piece of duct tape, a tube of lip balm, and one dandelion. A padlock bolts the grille doors over the wellhead. The lock is no bigger than the kind people use on a farm gate or a storage shed. This place did not spook me until I saw that frail padlock.

The dry summer wind soughs through the pine needles, bearing a mixed scent of pine, dust, and elk scat. The musky black pellets near the monument still shine with freshness, as if the elk had browsed here at dawn—chewing, dozing, staring incredulously at the metal plate riveted to the weathered concrete block.

Elk love this broken country. This time of year, they retire deep into the cool pines for shade and cover, then rally and feed in soft, grassy clearings like the one that surrounds me. There are signs of mule deer, too. Their pungent musk renders a tangible presence. We occupy the meadow alone, the elk and deer ghosts and I. The day will stay this way, with no other vehicle to pass save a pumper's, lunging toward town and a cold beer.

The sun bathes the clearing in photon-engorged light. Sleepy clouds of insects intoxicate themselves on the bright wildflowers. Out of hearing range: invisible currents of gas sucked out of the sandstone by relentless appetites, and the narcoleptic decay of tritium. To a lesser degree yet bearing the same irony as the White Sands Missile Range, this place mixes a marginal "wild" with massive human impact. I have come to it with the unnaturalist's eye, dragging along the usual bestiary to help sort out this geography of consequence, a Known Universe plump with anomalies.

The free-ranging mammalian anomaly in this country is a tawny sheep with a plush burst of mane from its throat to its knees. Against its hulk, native desert bighorns seem wiry and prissy, as ephemeral as an ancient petroglyph. As with the North American bighorns, this creature's agility on cliffs and rugged talus slopes bespeaks a near perfect union of muscle and flesh with terrain. Peer deep into its yellow eyes, and you will see not the deserts of the American Southwest but the coastal ranges and austere, arid expanses of North Africa.

Having demonstrated heat transfer to an inattentive audience of raucous piñon jays and ground squirrels, I sit down in the grass, not on the monument. Across my lap I spread the Map of the Known Universe and a photograph of a wild ram that appears to be in a highly sexual state.

The aoudad *(Ammotragus lervia)*, also known as Barbary sheep, once ranged from Morocco to the Red Sea. The slave-owning Tuaregs of the central Sahara hunted this sheep with dog packs and prized tents of its hide as the most elegant of shelters. In the early years of this century, American zoos purchased a number of aoudads. The North African native bred so well in captivity, zookeepers routinely fed excess aoudads to the zoos' carnivores.

Man comes to a wild landscape blinded, seeing not its own particularities but his own aims. The southwestern deserts have long been deemed lands in need of "correction." In the fifties New Mexicans believed they could correct nature's deficiencies by filling "empty" wild sheep niches with an edible, manageable, and, above all, sporting substitute. Thus, the same mind-set that studded the Jornada del Muerto with oryx from the Kalahari brought the aoudad to the American West. Fifty-six animals were released on the Canadian River north of Tucumcari. Six years later an unauthorized release by a hunters' group placed twenty-one aoudads in Canyon Largo, an extensive drainage several miles beyond the nuked meadow. Escapees from private game ranches ended up in pockets of habitat elsewhere in New Mexico.

The aoudads liked the territory. They thrived. The rams were promiscuous; the ewes commonly dropped twins. The New Mexican stock grew even larger in size class than their African brethren, fattened up on Gambel oak and mountain mahogany, the favored food of mule deer. Like the oryx, they did not always stay where wildlife managers wanted them to stay. As with the oryx, a simple strategy—ensuring that the exotics did not compete with domestic livestock, that predators did not compete with the hunters, and that nothing competed with the economic benefits of sport hunting—ultimately evolved into a carp-type problem.

The empty-niche theory no longer holds up against today's more enlightened wildlife biology, which favors native species in native habitats and considers exotics an irresponsible gamble. Exotics often outcompete natives for food and territory. They can alter plant communities, provide new hosts for disease and parasites, and, in some cases, attempt to interbreed with the natives.

Aoudads pose the greatest threat to the native desert bighorns that cling precariously to range in southern New Mexico. The state wildlife agency now kills any aoudad in occupied desert bighorn range, assuming it can be tracked down and shot. Introduced aoudads apparently made their own way to the San Andres Mountains; two were shot in the seventies, and there was a sighting (unconfirmed) in 1997, leaving the single ewe on the refuge above White Sands Missile Range in the wrong company. Liberal hunting policies "control" aoudads outside desert bighorn range, including the Canyon Largo herd, which despite sport harvest continues to expand north to Navajo Lake.

I study the healthy specimen of *Ammotragus lervia* in the photograph. The aoudad's lips curl back in the posture of the rut. He sports a thick mane under his chin and chaps of long hair behind his front legs. If a mighty Saharan sandstorm should blow across the page, he can bury his nose in his chaps. When his chaps grow too long—a teensy testosterone overload, perhaps—he will stumble over them.

The ram's neck bulges with the muscle needed to hold a curl of massive horns. Although the photograph does not show it, I have heard that mature rams must compensate for their horn mass when they turn their heads. If a ram turns his head too fast, the momentum can carry both head and headgear beyond the point where he intended to look. The thought makes me laugh out loud: a band of macho sheep flinging their heads toward me and coming up with an eyeful of empty desert air to my immediate right.

In the style of a petroglyph but with hairy leggings, I draw a herd of aoudads across the page of the Map. I give them sore necks. Like the weeds under the lizard's belly at home in Utah, this creature simply obeys its genes: cope, propagate, seek suitable habitat. Adaptive radiation on a global scale is an ancient story, dissimilar today only in style and degree. All of the world's wild sheep have a common ancestry. Some migrated from Asia to Europe and North Africa and became mouflon and aoudad; from Asia to North America to become mountain and desert bighorns. They came by hoof, and it took several thousand years to sort themselves out in their new geography. In contrast, the North African aoudad hitched a fast ride to the Known Universe. It took a few generations, some zoos, and a handful of private game ranches with safari delusions.

We may eventually run out of native desert bighorns. The aoudad may be better equipped to survive the world we have created. As we further change that world, we may forget we ever mourned a diminished native bestiary and start calling the weeds that replaced them our own. Someday we may sell New Mexican aoudad to the Moroccans to restock dwindling aoudad populations in the sub-Sahara. Suddenly the hairy sheep on my page grow a bit dizzy. They seem to be the supporting cast in a drama of outsized proportions, a drama of humans meddling and, in the end, outsmarting themselves completely. How very peculiar the Known Universe has become.

I will not find an aoudad here among the elk-nuzzled lupine and globemallow. They are downslope, in adjacent drainages, using a lower-elevation menu. No one can tell me how many aoudads occupy this edge of the Colorado Plateau or where—beyond general terms and sporadic, usually unconfirmed sightings—they roam. If, with your edited notions of proper native western wildlife, you come across one, you will likely react to its oddity in the same way you react to an atomic bomb under this woodland clearing. Neither quite fits the myth. Both taint the purist's notion of nature's wild garden. One—the enormous globule of unfinished physics—defies rational thought, so before you disintegrate with anxiety, you concentrate on the other, the sheep. It has fur. It breathes.

Should I seek the sheep or sleep with elk? For a moment I consider camping at Gasbuggy. This is, after all, a public national forest, where people pull clean mountain air into their lungs, sizzle their wienies or rehydrate their stroganoff over open-air pods of fuel, and maybe think for a moment about something besides the spouse that dumped them for a men's drumming circle instructor or the possibilities of being felled by *E. coli* or disgruntled postal workers.

Fragrant nests of pine needles along the meadow's fringe seduce me. I could spread my bag beneath one of the ponderosas, to which is attached a homey touch to ground zero: a small hand-built birdhouse. I like the tree's resolute skyward aim, its spicy, puzzle-piece bark. The ponderosa reminds me how ratty a desert rat I have become: I can walk up to a straight, tall tree and gawk. All the more reason to expand my horizons and stay here, I think—but only briefly. There is little doubt that elk or mule deer would wander into my sight at dusk and I could have these stately beasts all to myself, our hot-breathed mammal bodies bedded down beneath the stars, atop imported pieces of Tsé Valley's fossil river.

Geology is simultaneously the science of solidity and fluidity. It studies dead, inert rock and serves up clues to life itself. Lacking a geologist's eye, I cannot piece together the paleoenvironments— the Dakota and Cliff House sandstones, the Satan Tongue of Mancos Shale, the never-mapped lagoons of Cretaceous seas— beneath this pathetically tiny blob of concrete and bronze. I kneel down and lay my ear to the ground and listen. That is definitely not frijolium down there. Despite its antiquity, its seeming immutability, the earth's skin is somewhat of a mess in this part of the Known Universe—prodded, poked, piped, pumped, leached, scraped, stripped, stuffed with nitroglycerin and dreams of atomic kitchens. With consequences we likely underestimate, nature will take these intrusions into its own silent chemistry.

I came to Gasbuggy with the intention to bury my piece of yellow cake. But this is not the right place. The distance between my ear and the top of Gasbuggy's chimney-shaped puddle of radioactive matter is about 3,907 feet, several hundred feet above the point of detonation. Within that fractured rubble lies a ghost of a bomb more powerful than Trinity. Unlike Trinity, Gasbuggy showed its light to no one.

I never gave the complete text of Gasbuggy's bronze plaque. If you come to it, do not bring your backhoe. Hope that you can read, that you speak English.

PROJECT GASBUGGY

Nuclear explosive emplacement/Reentry Well (GB-ER)

Site of the first United States underground nuclear [a splat of bird poop over the *nu*] experiment for the stimulation of low-productivity gas reservoirs. A 29-kiloton nuclear explosive was detonated [squished bug] at a depth of 4,227 feet below this surface location on December 10, 1967.

No excavation, drilling, and/or removal of subsurface materials to a true vertical depth of 1,500 feet is permitted within a radius of 100 feet of this surface location nor any similar excavation, drilling, and/or removal of surface materials between the true vertical depths of 1,500 feet and 4,500 feet is permitted within a 600 foot radius of this surface location in the SE quarter of the SW quarter of section 36, T29N R4W New Mexico principal meridian, Rio Arriba County, New Mexico, without government permission.

United States Department of Energy—November 1978

The Last Cheater's Waltz

The black widow spiders wrapped the underside of my bicycle seat in gossamer condos and refused to budge. Several hummingbirds the size of a heartbeat collided full speed into the screenhouse mesh. Pinocchio beaks stuck in the small squares; they madly vibrated their wings in reverse and went nowhere. From the inside of the screenhouse, with the flat of my hand, I tried to punch them out of the vise without snapping off their beaks.

Like a troop of mobile mustaches, fuzzy brown caterpillars marched up the path from the screenhouse, ready to defoliate the nearest sapling. The coyotes yipped and yowled all night, and by day it rained lizards. Two hulking orange-headed spiny lizards chased and wrestled each other, scrambled up a cottonwood, then dropped at my feet when I passed. The lizards were brutish, muscular, and so inflated with reptilian machismo, you could strap one to each of your feet and skate off. Every evening a calico cat strolled through the high grass under the cottonwood grove. Actually, it was not a cat; it was a skunk with a rust-colored streak along its tail, a detail you might notice a bit too late after the cat mistake, along with the revelation that, around a skunk, a house with screen walls may not be an ideal refuge.

Our presence on this shaggy expanse of river valley appeared to be encouraging anarchy in the domestic wildlife. But that was not why I was running away from home.

My husband and his Navajo crew tackled our house construction with a fury. The building rose quickly from scraped red earth to rebar and concrete, from framed walls to roof trusses and sheath. The passive solar design was modest because we wanted a place that would entice sun and starlight, breezes and birds. The main events—desert, river, cliffs, canyons, mesas, and our incessant roamings in them—occurred outside the walls. All shelters require care (we called ours Paradise with Maintenance), although once occupied the house would remain dwarfed by the vast expanse of land around it, and we would look upon it with disbelief rather than possession. Its simplicity gave it the best sort of magnificence.

With few exceptions the construction ran smoothly. Despite a warning from one of the carpenters, we unearthed then reburied a pile of fluvial stones, the water-polished, spherical rubble of an old river channel. Once you expose the stones, you should leave them that way, the carpenter said. (Navajo superstition also says that you will suffer hip problems if you watch snakes mate, that whistling in the dark may summon ghosts, and that if you call yourself by your own name, your ears will dry up.) A few days after the warning, the carpenter rolled his pickup on the highway and a pipe wrench fell on Mark's head—minor injuries for both men, but thereafter any unburied stones stayed aboveground.

The medicine man who plumbed the house sang to each of his pipe welds. Because the Navajo consider it impolite to point with one's finger, the workers lifted their chins and raised their lips in the direction of whatever needed observation. Soon we, too, found ourselves pointing our lips at two-by-fours or rolls of duct tape or windows that needed shims. When I played classical music on the boom box, the crew told me it sounded like "shopping." Most of the time they listened to an AM station from Gallup, New Mexico—country-western music and a radio-savvy dialogue in rapid-fire Navajo, something like *Eh neh ish bih income tax preparation ya neh.* Mark and his helpers left for a weekend while I wrangled staple gun, heavy rolls of black roofing felt, and sacks of tin caps. I leaned too far into my work and stapled my hair to the roof. I did not mind because the desert spread below me in perfectly adulterous splendor and I had already decided to run away from home.

In town a flying wedge of mountain bikers, dressed in painted-on spandex body gloves mail-ordered from Bulgarian sex manuals, overshot their mecca to the north and ended up here, spreading the gospel of polymers and finding no converts in a land clearly devoid of granola and decent trails. An Army recruiter with a green face and head-to-toe camouflage handed out leaflets to Navajo teenagers. At the post office, where, from neighborly chats, I received the News of the World, the week's topics ran like this: the new dump, the old dump, political scandal in the Mosquito Committee, garden tomato varieties, the double rainbow everyone saw over the eastern mesas, and a communal hallucination over the imminent arrival of chain-hotel developers, with comment from all the requisite local parties—the we-want-to-get-rich faction, the sensible-growth faction, the over-my-dead-body faction.

Most of my neighbors were too busy blowtorching their goat-heads to talk to me about impending nuclear incineration. Mark turned comatose when I ranted about neutrinos or, with a sick, crepuscular grin, insisted on calling every meal *The Last Supper: Chili con Frijolium*. One morning he told me he wanted to take all my money, buy a Humvee, and "see the world." The next day he said he would really like to take tightrope-walking lessons. I attributed his state to epoxy fumes and sheetrock dust.

I freed hummingbirds. I dodged the thudding plop of wrestling lizards. My party calendar was empty. My head reeled with bombs. My decision was firm: to dismantle and relocate the Saint Thomas Aquinas Cactus and Succulent Society, to run away from home.

What binds a person to place? The Pueblo ancestors were tied to place by how far they could walk before starving. Today's reasons are more freely chosen. We are born somewhere and never consider leaving, or livelihood or family drew us, or in certain places, as people say about the West, the sex is better. To many, "environment" is a backdrop that wields irksome nuisances like floods or flat tires, or it is the strip of sky between buildings that reveals clues about the time of day.

"I may not know who I am but I know where I am from," Wallace Stegner said of his boyhood in Saskatchewan. His affections and prejudices, he claimed, were inscribed into his being by that prairie home. Each of us has a geography of character to match a physical geography—a curve of river, the evocative power of aridity, the way we respond to colors, weather, and light. When geography is earned, by ecological literacy, by truly knowing the inhabitants, history, and limits of one's home terrain, some new frontier arrives.

A boiled lizard inspired me to cross that frontier and deepen the knowledge. When I did, I precipitated not resurrection but a collapse of faith. Was I on the verge of an apostasy of place? The malaise of soul, so pervasive when I created its antidote, the Map, seemed incurable. The world hardened with the very antithesis of the sensual: underground pods of poison, vast tracts of nature preserved not by love but by the instruments of war, public rooms bursting with technology's glories and not a word, not a whisper, of its intentional designs on living beings. Out here in the red-boned desert, I once thought, the human voice seemed less consequential than in other places, at best a remote echo of intellectual ascetism. Now it was the only voice I heard, the desert itself an accomplice to betrayal.

Westerners are bred with a keen sense of kinship with the land and the certainty that it will never remain the same. Many of us carry the landscape as a rootless, half-baked nomadism, a displacement that feels singular although it is also a distinctly regional trait. Thus, fleeing the premises seemed more necessity than trauma. I entrusted the house construction to Mark's capable hands. I packed up the Map and camping supplies. To make my options amphibious, the whitewater raft went too, deflated and rolled up in the back of the truck, oars and aluminum frame strapped to the roof rack. I liberated one last hummingbird nose from the mesh and shut the screenhouse door behind me.

Partway up the path to the truck, I discovered a spiny lizard sticking straight out of sand flattened by a truck tire. Somehow the lizard had escaped a fatal crushing; somehow it had dug itself out of its tomb, but only partially. From head to "waist" the upper body was free. Tail and hind legs still lay pinned beneath the dirt. The earthen trap propped it up like a tent stake. It flailed about in a pathetic pivot, forelegs thrashing the air, growing weaker and weaker, like a toy whose batteries were about to expire. As I leaned down to dig it out, I swore I saw flared nostrils and the whites of tiny terrified eyes. Liberated, the lizard slowly crawled under a rabbitbrush, its tail nearly severed close to the base—not a minor injury. I walked on to the truck, leaving the lizard to recover.

Because bars in rural Utah are about as common as tattoos on a polar bear's lip, it is often difficult to find professional help. En route to the as-yet-unspecified Wherever that I was running to, luck brought both.

"Show me what you've got," said my professional adviser, a geologist with a number of empty beer glasses on the table in front of him. The view from the bar window took in a slender span of steel bridge over the river and a jumbled cliff of Halgaito Shale in a distinct brick red called *halchíí* in Navajo.

I plunked down the blob of yellow cake. Even after considerable time and miles in the back of the truck, including a round-trip to Los Alamos, the rock had not yet scorched a hole through the pickup bed and liquefied the driveshaft. I figured it would take a while to defrost the tabletop. The rock appeared small and somewhat ordinary, rather like a petrified pineapple. The canary yellow glow, so vibrant when I had discovered the rock below the abandoned highway alongside our property, seemed to have faded. Nevertheless, I braced myself for the geologist's verdict: your dreamland on the San Juan River sits on a uranium dump, he might conclude, or, as they drove to the distant processing mill, nearly every ore hauler during the mining boom had flung these rogue Day-Glo nuggets out the window on the chance that one day a couple of spongiform eco-puffs might settle there.

"What we're looking for are metallic elements compounding

with the vanadate radical," my friend explained. He ordered two beers. So far so good, I thought. If we were looking at Chernobyl *sur la table*, he would have ordered ten. He ran a hand lens over the rock's surface, carefully examining a lumpy stretch of grayish aggregates.

Beyond the window the bridge spanned the river canyon like a plank laid across a steep-sided ditch. The AEC, patron saint of local "autonomy," picked up the tab for the steel bridge— and for most of the roads in the region—in the late fifties. Before that, herds of sheep and vehicles hauling uranium ore used an old cable bridge, whose weight limit was determined experientially. A heavily loaded truck tilted so far downhill as the bridge sank with its weight, the driver lost sight of his hood ornament, local legend said. At the lowest point of the sag, he either plunged into the river, and everyone would know that the weight limit had been exceeded, or he drove uphill on a grade so steep, he could not see the bridge planks ahead of him.

A woman who had grown up in that era described the time she crossed the bridge in an ore hauler driven by her brother. At the bridge's maximum sag point the truck's rear wheels crashed through the boards. " 'Run!' my brother screamed, and I did, like hell, to the wrong side of the river," she told me. Her brother stood safely on the opposite bank; the truck remained stuck in the middle of the bridge between them. "They dumped the load of uranium ore into the river and winched the truck out of the hole. It happened all the time. A lot of hot rock went into the San Juan."

To yield a small quantity of semirefined uranium oxide, the material that is then enriched for weapons, ore processing leaves behind literally tons of bulk and most of the glow. A ton of raw ore yields about four pounds of uranium oxide—think of extracting a couple of jumbo lemon wafers from a stone pyramid. According to the U.S. Department of Energy, uranium tailings make up the largest volume of any category of radioactive waste in the country: about 27 million tons. Most of the tailings piles were abandoned during the mining bust, and all of them last a very long time. The radionuclide thorium, for example, has a half-life of 77,000 years, although radon gas and groundwater contamination are considered the immediate health threats.

When mined ore entered the mill that once stood across the river from the bar, about 99 percent of it came out as waste—an earthen residue of fine sand, which the gusty desert winds blew all over the place. The waste contained 85 percent of the radioactivity present in the processed ore. For thirty-seven years most of these tailings slumped toward the river, to depths of forty feet.

In the early nineties, cleanup operations consolidated four million cubic yards of waste inside an enormous cell, then capped it with a thick layer of clay, gravel, and crushed limestone. This tomb, which sits on a terrace above the river on the Navajo side of the bridge, also holds radioactive building materials from nearby houses. After nearly four decades of off-and-on occupancy by mill workers and local Navajo families, the houses were demolished and buried because their foundations had been built with tailings from the old mill.

The recent cleanup operations hauled truckload after truckload of mine and mill tailings from Tsé Valley, an activity that accounted for the "superhighway" and earthworks that I had encountered on my search for claret cup cacti. The water hole enclosed within the flimsy fence likely served as a leach pond. The bulk of Tsé's hazardous waste disappeared beneath the limestone cap long after its desired goods had been exported to the far-flung vortexes of bomb alchemy.

A number of these tailings cells dot the Colorado Plateau. Their caretakers assuage our fears with a cavalier befuddlement. The tailings, they say, which for fifty years were not harmful, are less not-harmful now that they are in *long-term* (do not dig here until A.D. 10,000) *isolation* (state-of-the-art precautions taken against groundwater leakage). We hear that certain mine wastes are so harmless, we can *eat* the stuff; then they pack the stuff into million-dollar megabunkers surrounded by chain-link fence and razor wire.

Am I the only one around here who is worried sick about these hot slabs of cold war detritus? The slowing of the doomsday clock has tendered apathy and a relief that people will not surrender easily. Few would return to the amorphous dread of nuclear anxiety, so absorbed are we in dreads with seemingly greater odds: cancer, heart disease, cerebral hemorrhage, bombs placed on airplanes for ideological purposes. Locust plagues and dire loneliness. Leaky breast implants, a diminishing supply of world sperm, electrocution by one's turbo-powered tie rack. Fascists with Web sites. The frightening biological dystopia of the global economy. Planetary decline not by a couple of H-bombs but by the slow-cook of greenhouse gases and shredding ozone layers.

Outside the bar, the river glistened in the afternoon sun. Inside, people laughed, gossiped, and talked about their horses. Few in the crowd realized they were knocking back Bud Light a stone's throw from a Superfund site. Nor did they want some fugitive apostate like me to unpack the century's darker history. One prefers one's monuments to be like Gasbuggy, surrounded by elk and tansy mustard. I was on my own with the toxic pineapple and whatever it boded for the land beneath the lizard's belly.

Left untouched in its Mesozoic beds, the mineral carnotite, known commonly as yellow cake, does not do much. Plucked from the sandstone and milled, it yields radium, vanadium, and uranium, an element with a monster of an atom, a bloated nucleus, and the seeds of humanity's demise. *Ouranos,* I daydreamed, Greek for "heaven" and the name of a planet with fifteen moons. Pluto, Greek god of the dead, a one-mooned planet and namesake of Trinity and Nagasaki's plutonium hearts. A species that regards itself as very important gives both celestial and earthly matter the names of deities.

"Vanadium was discovered in Sweden," I remarked out loud, should my geologist friend be dying to share the constellation of ironies inherent in his task. "*Vanadis* is Latin for the Scandinavian goddess of love."

"*Asphaltos,*" he neologized, "with a Greek root in *sphaleros,* which more or less means 'something that trips or deceives.' *A* plus *sphalt* is 'not tripping' or 'not falling' and probably refers to a substance once used to reinforce walls."

The dead languages wafted into the airwaves, joining animated bubbles of Navajo and western twang around us. Our conversation stung into motion a molecule of incredulity that quickly inflated into a suffocating blimp of stupidity. "Asphalt?" I peeped.

He looked at me as one might look at a recalcitrant beagle, poised to pet me on the benign space between my ears. "What you have here is your basic gravel-pit granola mixed with a petroleum product. The only way you could make a bomb out of it would be to climb up a very tall ladder and drop it on someone's head."

He slapped the rock. "It's bitumen in a solid state, formed by the evaporation of volatiles from petroleum. Also known as asphalt," he continued. "The yellow is sun-aged, vintage chemical paint commonly used to distinguish passing and no-passing zones on land-based transportation corridors. You've got mostly no-passing—lots of yellow." He called for more beer.

"Your yellow cake is a chunk of old highway."

. . .

Dr. Freud might say that Thanatos is running amok among baby boomers like me, whose middle age feels like a sudden abduction to Planet Mortality and incites compulsive shopping for inner lives as if there was no tomorrow. Friends might say that land-mining the neighborhood and my psyche with atomic bombs displaces a fear of death and—why not?—makes it cataclysmic. Heidegger might say that human life is only lived authentically when one is aware of the presence of death, that without this there is only the impoverished rubbish of materialism. Perhaps one chooses to live in the desert because it lays bare this authenticity. Along with its spare and sensuous beauty, it always deals a wild card.

Everyone is born to die. Human pride inclines us to think of that death as our own, a prospect I happen to feel most acutely on commercial airliners. Yet as I slogged through the bog of nuclear doomsday, death in the Known Universe grew less and less personal. It was as if we humans were so incapable of imagining the absolute end, of our species and this planet, we had deliberately constructed it, once and for all, for every last one of us. As Hans Koning wrote in a 1997 *Atlantic Monthly* essay, "[O]ur repressed fear [of atomic holocaust], destroying one more illusion of humanity (its continuity), must have done great damage to our common psyche."

As I aimed my repressed fears toward Wherever, I doubted that the end would come flying in from Siberia in the carapaces of pointy-nosed lozenges of steel, leaving me about twelve minutes to do something about it. The pixie dust of the only nuclear war thus far—the bombing of the American West—may or may not cause my demise. The land under the lizard's belly and the greater environs of the Known Universe were not toxic waste dumps but the geography of a broader legacy, an abused, outback colony of the cold war. Nevertheless, I felt as if someone's tire had squished half of me. I wanted to crawl under a rabbitbrush, determined to never again return to that barbaric patch of injuring ground.

As I left the bar I took a long, loving look at the river. I had the raft. I could inflate it, rig it, ride it all the way to Mexico, bumping down a staircase of dams as a lunatic might ride the wake-up rumble strip on the edge of a highway. But the raft stayed in the truck, a rolled-up, endomorphic blob of endless pleasure and miraculous petrochemistry, its skin manufactured by the same company that makes the sheathing on the Stealth bomber, the coating that helps the aircraft deflect radar.

The bar was twenty miles from home. My destination, evolving from an ill-defined instinct, seemed to be the enormous mesa that floated on the horizon, several miles distant. As I left the river behind, I caught glimpses of blue-gray between bloodred hills: the brand-spanking-new uranium tailings pile. It sprawled over the cusp of a dry wash, a seemingly endless field of limestone boulders surrounded by a chain-link fence. Against the almost lurid red rock, it gave the bizarre sensation of a solidified lake. Heat waves rose from its surface into a quivering mirage.

Apostasies of place do not come without difficulties. David James Duncan wrote, "One of the harsh but deep consolations of watching a loved homeplace slip away from you is that, without the loved home, you're suddenly naked enough to feel the blood, begging direction."

I tried to put the gray wedge and the Known Universe at my back. That is the trouble with maps, I thought. Sometimes you come to an edge that simply breaks off.

Is *reptile heart* an oxymoron? Does the reflexive anthropomorphism of the top mammal, warm-blooded and able to generate heat from within our own bodies, ascribe cold-heartedness to the cold-blooded?

The world is a lizard's furnace. An elongated body soaks up radiant heat from the sun and from sun-warmed surfaces of stone and sand: dark along the spine for heat absorption, pale belly for heat reflection. After fall's first frost my home tribe of side-blotched lizards will emerge as if dyed, their sheath of skin turned deep umber to absorb more heat. By day's peak they lighten up. There are night lizards as well (family Xantusiidae), crepuscular or diurnal though crevice-dwelling, secretive, and fond of spiders.

Warm-bloodedness allows for migration; mammals take along their steady body temperature despite the whims of environment.

To mammals, hair and fur are special—transfiguring and sensitive to touch. No matter that scales are related to hair, nothing will convince us that reptiles are cuddly. Does a lizard, then, have a heart? In the sense of that robust metaphor of compassion and warmth, you would have to ask another lizard. What we see when we cut open the little tuna-flavored scudders are two separate aortic trunks, but, unlike mammal hearts, the lizard heart mixes venous and arterial blood to some extent because the heart's single ventricle is not fully divided by a partition. A lizard heart serves the gods of thermoregulation. A lizard brain resembles a bird's. A lizard's smile looks like cynicism.

On the Map of the Known Universe, beneath the small heart of the side-blotched lizard that I set on the center of my world, lay an enormous tableland, a middle world between an island of lofty mountains and the open, broken desert that sprawls toward Arizona. The mesa's pelt of piñon and juniper trees is as much a mature forest as ponderosa and fir on a mountain slope. It is the high desert's climax woodland, and it blocks the view, giving the sensation of an uncreased, slow carpet of dark green. Yet when you set out across these flats, you will soon come to what travelers long before you called a cruel joke. From one end to the other the mesa is carved with deep, often impassable canyons. They begin with the shallowest depressions and the most western of names—wash, arroyo, draw—then cleave, often abruptly, into chasms with perpendicular walls several hundred feet high and bewildering courses that end up cutting the mesa into pieces.

I first came to the mesa nearly twenty years before. It was not my destination but words on a road map, a formal graphic notation of a place that I planned to pass through during a trip from Montana to California. On that trip I pulled off the road to stretch my legs among the mesa's piñons and junipers. I stayed a month.

The mesa grows an abundance of herbal plants significant to the Navajo. Medicine men and women still bring patients here to cure them of loneliness and sorrow. In retrospect, however, I do not believe that a condition of mind spurred the walkabout and made me four weeks late for California. It was the mesa itself that drew me. An involuntary tropism bent me toward its warmth and light. The land's most daunting qualities quickly took hold of all affection. As Mary Austin wrote, "They trick the sense of time, so that once inhabiting there you always mean to go away without quite realizing that you have not done it."

A friend would later describe this place as annoyingly indefinite. "There is no 'there' there," he said. On the contrary, it is *all* there, an exquisite ubiquity that for me integrated senses and emplacement perfectly. As I roamed the mesa for that first month, I borrowed these words, their origin lost: Here is a place, which given enough time, sun, and acquaintance, could come perilously close to transcendence.

Over the years, I came back to the mesa again and again, from my home in Montana and eventually from closer locales when I moved to southern Utah permanently. My sojourns took up all of the free time I could muster, and my hikes lasted as long as my food supply, which was in turn measured by the water available in the canyons and the weight I could carry on my back. My clothes and skin acquired a red tint, the color of the sandstone. I blew out hiking boots and knee cartilage. Camping became like a much-practiced art, pulled together by a decent knife and tasks stripped down to a purity of motions. In those days I looked over my shoulder for the cement mixers and recreation-crazed hordes on the horizon. Yet I seldom encountered other people.

Solitude, in fact, became for me an aesthetic sensation. Ever since I can remember I have lived alone, and quite well, inside my own head. The spare desert stirred the most luxuriant imaginings; shadow and color bore meaning, light a deliriously languid ecstasy that felt like being touched. Often there would come to me mysteries more intriguing than any lucidity—how, for instance, in a place with few or no human beings, one could begin to see the worth of what it means to be human. Solitude tempered an inquietude; it settled the taste of restlessness enough to allow me to slow down and take responsibility for my own well-being. Ironically, the attraction to this landscape also resembled an outlaw coupling, the wild anarchy of a love affair whose heated obsession betrayed and unraveled some other, weaker fidelity. I risked social and professional obligations, and my loved ones' patience, simply to submit to an involuntary hunger for light, rock, and air.

On the mesa springtime's scourge of biting gnats often covered my skin with flaming bumps. On one backcountry journey the inflammation grew so intolerable, I cleaned up (solar shower) and trimmed my hair (Leatherman Super Tool) to the style of a comatose yucca plant, then drove forty miles to the nearest town. I staggered about like one of those Florida alligators who, for no apparent reason—parasites in the brain, perhaps—crawls in from the bayou and starts lunging and ripping off car bumpers.

I found a pharmacy and begged for cooling lotions and lethal insecticides. I subjected the pharmacist, an aloof, indoors sort of man, to the incoherent monologue of an isolated person. "I'm out on the mesa," I babbled. "Pinheaded bugs have made my skin a continent of tiny, active volcanoes."

On a yellow plastic tray he segregated an allotment of fuchsia capsules and plinked them into a cup. The lurid colors screamed placebo. When he spoke, his tone of vinyl sincerity instantly revealed two things: I had thistles for brains, and he hated me. After all, we nature buffs, when we were not too busy trying to decide what sex to be, had brought mining, logging, ranching, and the military-industrial complex to their knees.

"How do I stop this misery?" I groaned, scanning the shelves for a cure.

"Don't go out there," he said flatly.

I contemplated this reasonable observation for about sixteen seconds. Move to town. Hang out at the laundromat. Have eight children. Then I melted back into the piñon-juniper forest. Thereafter, supply runs were committed with utmost stealth.

And now I was on the mesa for the four-thousandth time. Surprisingly, I cannot map it because every time I am here I become mildly lost. Lost, of course, is the ultimate metaphor of discovery. Fairly quickly you find out who you are and what you can do; you feel keenly the pulse of your own endeavors. In few other situations does the dialogue between the internal and external landscapes run so intensely. After losing home there can be no better condition than to be lost again.

The canyon exhaled robust aromas of foliage and soil moist from heavy monsoon rains. Along the narrow wash through the canyon bottom, water still flowed. Crystal clear, it whispered over slickrock, then danced down ledges that layered like folios of a book. In pools its depth acquired the color of emeralds. I conformed my own motion to the canyon's sinuosity—sweeping fins of sandstone, one curve after the other—and in doing so crossed the stream many times. Voluminous white clouds passed over the canyon rims, their undersides blushing with the rose-colored reflection of the land beneath them. I walked alternately on slickrock or in water, in shadow or in sunlight.

Here and there patches of purple aster nestled in rock crevices, and lanky horsetail ferns along the stream made a shaggy meadow of the banks. Indian paintbrush threw a spark of crimson against the silver-green of sage and rabbitbrush. Cottonwood and hackberry found ample underground moisture to give them the breadth and height of stately trees. It has been said that an involuntary hunger for greenness lies in the hearts of desert lovers. I fed on the ever faithful: Gambel oak, squawbush, ricegrass, threadleaf groundsel, claret cup, prickly pear, and other plants as familiar as my own hands and feet.

The rain-fed luxuriance implied an uninhabited jungle. Yet like other canyons that slice the mesa, this one also harbored a series of discrete villages. In the cliffs above I spotted masonry storage cists tucked into impossible cracks of sandstone with no apparent access. For the past several nights I had slept within sight of prehistoric structures. Some were roughly contemporary with the Basketmakers of my backyard burial. Others fell into the later Pueblo phases, as archaeologists arrange them, dating back more than a thousand years.

After living here so long, a strange paradox has taunted my curiosity. On one side, the compelling desire to see and know every last Anasazi site in the Known Universe. On the other, a striving to live within deep history gracefully and intuitively, to take my humble place inside the neighborhood's overlays of time. At first glance the canyons look unmarked. Then patterns emerge, not just in paintbrush or coral sand laced into ripples by the wind, but as organized forms of human thought. You see a stone house, then ten more. You notice corn husks tied in elegant knots and sherds of clay painted black and white or impressed with the whorls of a fingertip. You remember a burial toad. Then all of the patterns meld and from exhalation and inhalation rather than conscious intent comes the sumptuous irony of a single, vibrant continuity of humankind in this harsh and precarious desert.

At the junction of a tributary canyon, I paused to examine a lively band of rock art on a freestanding boulder. Desert varnish, the patina of hardened minerals that formed the artist's medium, darkened the boulder's surface to the color of dried blood. The petroglyphs flew across the rock face as if shot from a cannon and frozen astride an arc of air. A horned anthropomorph with a scorpion attached to its toe, knobbed poles, and spidery grids lay on their sides. Bighorn sheep teetered on their noses; snakes stood on their tails. Erosion likely weakened the boulder's pediment until it toppled, turning the petroglyphs on their sides.

The bighorn sheep traversed the rock face in a dense cluster, together in art as in life. From birth, lambs will follow a lead ewe to food and water holes used by generations, establishing a fixed sheep-group life that unravels only under extreme pressure. Although rams may travel solo, most bighorns live in small bands, ewes with their lambs and yearlings, juvenile rams in bachelor bands that feed, rest, and occasionally let each other have it in a ritual bonking of heads. Alarmed, the herd vanishes as one— hundreds of pounds of flesh and horn and hoof lost like smoke in steep wrinkles of rock. Bighorns nuzzle and crowd one another, swinging their sleek rumps. The rams strut and lift their chins and thirty vain pounds of headgear, expecting admiration. Bighorn sheep bleat, grunt, and growl; they become famously belligerent and flare their nostrils and bulge their eyes. They are the most gregarious of species. It is impossible to imagine a single wild sheep, only one sheep short of zero sheep. No mate, no touch, no mirror of one's own curious amber eyes.

I dropped my pack and took the time to sketch the bighorn sheep petroglyphs. I finished one animal, then went no further. The bare white space of the page surrounded the spindly lines of ink like 58,000 acres of empty New Mexico mountains. Here on my paper was San Andres Ewe 067. She was so lonely. I began to weep.

As usual I was mildly lost, and as usual I did not mind. "Upcanyon" was a safe bet. The rims defined the route; the day's requirement was to take this simple journey, one foot in front of the other. "A walk expresses space and freedom and the knowledge of it can live in the imagination of anyone, and that is another space, too," wrote British artist Richard Long. "A walk traces the surface of the land, it follows an idea. . . . The place of a walk is there before the walk and after it." My walk traced a surface that indeed elicited an inert eternity, even as gravity wore it down. Voluptuously weathered escarpments retreated from the canyon floor, spalling stones too small to dimple the ground and boulders so enormous, they half buried themselves like menhirs when they fell.

I found the night's camp, an alcove about seventy feet above the canyon bottom, chosen for its lack of dwellings and artifacts. It was a spare cove of shelter under an arch of rock, with a sweeping view of potential invaders and a flat sandy floor on which to sleep. I extricated myself from backpack and the waffle-soled torture chambers that imprisoned my feet. I had eaten most of the pack's weight. The remaining tonnage included dinner, breakfast, and enough water for the next morning's half-day hike to the head of the canyon and my truck.

While I was not paying attention, someone plundered the tendons and stamina of the *peregrina* who wandered these rugged canyons all those years. Now I achieved forward motion with pathetic whimpers for the services of a chiropractor. When I sat down on a makeshift lounge arranged with pack and wadded-up shirt, I spent a moment wondering if I would ever be able to get up again. I decided that I probably would not, but when the time came I could grovel nicely across the sand and fall facedown on the sleeping bag. In the meantime I settled in with a mug of spicy tea and watched the last sunlight's glory. It torched the piñons and junipers on the canyon rims and illuminated the alcove's interior with a thick apricot light—the light, I thought as I basked in it, that slickrock would make if it were translucent.

I ate a monkish repast, then indulged in a rare treat: an incense fire. With dry grass and juniper twigs, I built it dutifully small, in my tin dinner plate. Yemeni women burn herbs and hold their clothes and hair in the smoke to scent them. This I did with the sweet aromatics of juniper.

I was grateful to be lost in the wrong canyon. I did not wish to retire for the night with war on the mind. In another canyon, higher into the mesa than I planned to go, lay a site that cast light on the most elusive qualities of southwestern prehistory: behaviors of passion. There, in the cusp of an alcove larger than mine, excavations uncovered a burial older and more extensive than the midden at the end of my driveway. Its contents were disturbing and so, too, the act of exhuming them, the equivalent of a team of Indian archaeologists excavating Arlington National Cemetery to obtain information about bone structure, diet, jewelry, buttons, dental hygiene, and social hierarchies.

Whereas the driveway midden held scant but typical burial goods—pots, shrouds, animal bits, and other assemblages of peace and sorrow—knives, bone daggers, darts, and other weapons dominated the mass burial upcanyon from my camp. The excavators found points embedded in backbones, arrows shot through breastbones, hipbones skewered by an obsidian blade four inches long, broken heads, broken arms, broken ribs, broken jaws.

The nature of the injuries and the number of skeletons (more than ninety) implied ritual execution rather than battle. Archaeologists speculate that most of the people interred at this site, possibly 80 percent, died from stabbing, bludgeoning, and other traumatic wounds inflicted at close range. Most of the dead, but not all, were male. A number of skeletons were randomly heaped, intriguing archaeologists with the possibility that the heapers were a social group different from the heapees. In other words, the survivors buried their own with care but threw their assailants into a pit.

Until recently southwestern ethnologists skirted the issue of episodic violence among the ancient Puebloans, whom most people prefer to think of as pleasantly pacifist agriculturists in yucca sandals, with gorgeous pottery and magnificently enigmatic rock art. However, numerous sites in the Four Corners region reveal patterns of conflict in this complex culture, ascribing to it a fuller range of humanness. Like us, they were splendid beings and cruel brutes. Was their aggression directed at outsiders or between neighbors or within a clan? How frequently did hostilities occur? Was the massacre upcanyon from this camp a form of social control—killing individuals to keep the group whole? If so, the Anasazi would not be the only society to punish others for breaches of acceptable behavior or grave threats to the group's well-being.

Less than three hundred years ago, peace-loving Pueblos to the south killed the inhabitants of one of their own villages to purge religious corruption brought in by a group of strangers who built a church, "washed heads," preached hell, and so divided the people from their traditions. The village was destroyed. In the eyes of the destroyers, it had lived out its life. The village has been deserted ever since, and until I stood on it, surrounded by stone rubble, broken pots, arrowheads, and the corn offerings of anonymous visitors, no sound but the wind off the mesas lifting my hair, I did not know what "deserted" meant.

My visits to the White Sands Missile Range and Los Alamos showed me the cryogenic detachment of modern military technology. Stalking by programmed drones, death by floppy disk— *things* do the work of killing, allowing combatants to destroy people whose humanity is well out of range. What happens to courage when the warrior becomes a technician? The Anasazi bones reveal the sheer intimacy of conflict. Bones document egregious injury. Compassion and laughter do not break jaws or drive a stone blade into someone's rib cage. No matter how intently you explore Anasazi country, you may never find physical evidence of patience or boredom or benevolence, of a palm stroking the face, a hand on the shoulder for reassurance or pride. Yet here in my alcove, where blue dusk has come swiftly down, followed by that particular desert silence that hovers before the full night, it was to these invisible gestures that I was drawn.

Another cup of tea in hand, candle lit beside me, I opened the Map of the Known Universe and began a list. How am I like these ancient desert dwellers? I asked. What universal human traits do we share? Consciousness, I wrote, a shared architecture of the mind. I lived in the Age of Deep Space, but I made this list with a Stone Age brain. Language, I noted next, including grunts, singing, and baby talk. Memory. Gossip. Mourning. Crying. That torrid nest of green flames, jealousy. Giggles. Frowns. Sticking out your tongue. Recognizing other faces. The pleasure of someone else's fingers in your hair. A fondness for sweetness? Not sure about that one. Dreaming. Dancing. Forming mental maps so we can find our way home or hunt or drive a bus. An inclination to divide the world into Us and Them and find pretexts to tear Them to pieces.

C. S. Lewis once looked inside his thoroughly twentieth-century self and found "a zoo of lusts, a bedlam of ambitions, a nursery of fears, a harem of fondled hatreds." On my list I noted the bedlams and harems, but they made my body feel like cement so I added altruism and emotional solace. I traded tea for a hip flask of cheap, throat-burning whiskey. Outside the candle's aura, night seeped from the sandstone, carrying with it the silence of a kiva.

Where in all of this was beauty? Is beauty not at the bare core of all things? Do people ever feel like fighting when they are engrossed in a state of wonder? Does life not present a full measure of magnificence and terror—*tso'ya* and *attanni*, beauty and danger? On the Map of the Known Universe I drew pictures of physicists snipping cables at Trinity so they might revel in the sheer miracle of the thirty-eight-millionth year of toad copulation. Everyone halting everything, merely to listen to Tchaikovsky's waltz. Missiles crippled by aesthetic essences. Just as I imagined the entire Nevada Nuclear Test Site turned over to poets, my candle sputtered and died, plunging me into blackness.

The hushed severity of the slickrock chasm thickened. Time was ripe for a bit of blue fog or a wolf shriek. I stood up and started to move in a slow, waltzing rhythm. A Navajo friend once told me that his people do not sin. Rather, they are "out of order." I liked the way that "out of order" implied a sense of mechanical failure as well as a misalignment with all of nature. Only when someone was in a sacred situation, at a sing or ceremonial, my friend said, was harmony restored, and even then, residue remained outside the ceremonial membrane, usually in the form of ghosts, so you had to keep singing, all your life. Perhaps the right steps would put me back in order and, while I was at it, set the Known Universe right. Either that, or I would dance off the alcove's lip and fall headfirst into a prickly pear cactus.

During a lifetime spent outdoors I have encountered a good share of potentially aggressive creatures, and most of them treated me with indifference. To those that would fear me, I appear unthreatening. To those that would eat me, I arouse no appetite. A black bear once lumbered into the tarp lean-to in which I dozed and licked my whiskey cup. The cougars have been several, including one that leaped over me in my bed on a riverbank, and another that lounged on a boulder, tail switching and forelegs outstretched in a library lion recline, following my progress up the switchback trail below its perch. Bighorn sheep have taken me into their routine so comfortably, they nap when I nap. In river camps, toads seem content to squat by my feet, and my toes will often attract whipsnakes—elongated, creeping digestive tracts with slender, darting tongues that collect my scent molecules from the air, then bring them to the sensory mass on the roof of their mouths to tell them if I am edible or mate-able.

Perhaps these creatures sense a kind of innately feral pacifism. I harbor no Saint Francis of Assisi delusions, no claim to psychic bioesoterica via mute interspecies neurotransmitters, nor would I test my "impunity" in the presence of a grouchy grizzly bear. Around wild creatures, with no conscious effort whatsoever, I simply seem to be wallpaper. So when the thin, silvery creature slipped past me in the alcove, I was not alarmed.

A kit fox is a diminutive, almost catlike canid, buff and grayish, with exceptionally long ears that disperse body heat and pivot like radar detectors. It is neither rare nor timid. On tall, spindly legs, this one trotted resolutely by as if it were late for church. Where the kit fox brushed past me, my skin burned. The rest of my body became like smoke. *Don't go out there,* I thought with a laugh as I dropped down to hands and knees and crawled across the sand and into my bed.

Then I slept the long, deep mammalian sleep that sets the mind's waves close to the earth's own quivering frequency. Epics unfurled across my brain. Unsuppressed by the normal vision of waking hours, the images fluoresced wildly from the eye of the spirit. In one episode of dreams I loped through an open desert, grabbed armfuls of baby kit foxes, then clambered to the roof of a glossy black stretch limo to save the fox cubs from a horde of hungry bears. A low-slung sun outlined every shape in warm, golden light. I felt no fear, only a slow dilation of patience. All around us the bears drooled and clacked their teeth. The little kit foxes dug their claws into my skin and yipped for dear life.

Imagine this: one capsized apostate, standing on the edge of the mesa, poised to fling the Map of the Known Universe off a sheer, thousand-foot-high cliff.

The mesa's piñon-juniper forest retreated short of the dizzying precipice as if anticipating the free-fall into thin air. The last stand of scattered trees left only a gentle undulation of bare slickrock to stretch to the brink. Behind me, well back from the edge, the truck sat at the end of the dirt road that led to the promontory. On this wide-open point of land the highest objects were the oar pins on the raft frame, which I had strapped to the roof rack for the run-away's contingency of river travel. The steel posts jutted into a vast sky. From the stereo a waltz drifted into the ethos of a hundred-mile view deep into the Known Universe. Sunlight bathed the mesa, though an enormous mass of clouds weighed down the far-thest horizon in dark indigo.

I held the sketchbook firmly, as if my fingers and palms could feel the earth's gravity through them. Tchaikovsky's waltz incited, as a waltz should, a heady state, a precarious union of delirium and control.

For nearly twenty years in this red-boned desert, I have always known the *walzen*, the turning, to be passionate and obsessive. It had all the trappings of a biological imperative, an innate engage-ment with environment that asserted itself in varying degrees of physical intensity, from the most reflexive movement through its spaces to the sheer panic of dislocation, when, off the map, on various travels, I felt *place* acutely by its absence. Those who cross the ocean change their sky but not their soul, the axiom says.

On the Colorado Plateau, with its considerable share of wild-lands, a natural world more or less intact, the most exotic terrain may be the plateau's own history. During my recent journeys this history felt foreign and unnervingly off-the-Map, even as I lived in its heart. Gaze out from the mesa, and you will meet my duplici-tous lover. You will see eternity, a desert that like no other place exudes the timelessness of nature as the final arbiter. Scrape off our century, and you will find its usurper, pressed into a nugget of inorganic matter, the single greatest threat to the continuity of life. This history inscribed itself on the Map's most alarming folios; ignoring it was no way to earn Home. The past is at its best, wrote historian William Chapman in *Preserving the Past,* "when it takes us to places that counsel and instruct, that show us who we are by showing us where we have been, that remind us of our connection to *what happened here.*" (Italics his.)

The incongruous geography of eternity and apocalypse began in a windswept valley on Navajo land, visible from my perch on the mesa. On one perimeter a rough sandstone escarpment spilled talus and claret cup cactus to the valley floor. Broken from its skin were chunks of fossil rivers, mined and exported for watch dials, medical aids, dinner plates, and a mineral named for a love goddess. Rubble from the mines remained behind in waste piles at various sites in the Four Corners region. Then the world shifted, and one era's waste became another's weapon.

Tsé Valley's ore joined similar extractions from deepest Africa and the boreal zones of northern Canada, then disappeared into the industrial digesters of the Manhattan Project. Its elixir was fashioned into bullet-shaped cores and dense globes of a metal admired for its tactile warmth and its ability to adopt different crystalline structures, each with its own behavior. For at least two sets of hemispheres of this metal, the desired behavior was clearly demarcated. One set went to central New Mexico during a hot week in July, with everyone cursing the desert. The other went to Japan, preceded by its bullet-core mate.

The Map of the Known Universe showed me that the earth around Trinity, Gasbuggy, Nevada, and other ground zeroes held alien pebbles—pieces of the Tsé Valley's fossil rivers. I had a final entry, however.

My pen floated smoothly over the page, filling empty space in the Known Universe with bits of Triassic point bars and channel sediments from my beloved homeland. From the air these pieces of Home took forty-three seconds to reach Hiroshima, a fraction less to reach Nagasaki.

From this lofty height I saw the serrated Tsé k'aan anticline and below it a faint glimpse of Tsé Valley. No tourists roamed it; no monument marked it with the blood of several hundred thousand people. To the west rose Naatsis'áán—Navajo Mountain—capped with a headdress of blue-black thunderheads. Distant mesas rode the horizon like curtains of washed silk. Below me I traced the veins and arteries of washes that flowed into the ventricle of the San Juan River. I looked down on every rock and boulder that I would struggle with if I were on the ground, afoot. From here there was no uphill. Ravens showed me their backs. A blazing cataract of reds exploded without a sound. Only a hard squint could swallow the distances.

The target presented itself, a blue-cornmeal tortilla slapped across bloodred toxic rock, holding back the heat. My plan was to toss the Map off the mesa, aiming it at the uranium tailings pile, that broad, glow-in-the-dark, bluish-gray wedge set down in the heart of the world's most beautiful Universe, insane and forever.

The trouble with this plan was that I forgot I have brain-screeching vertigo.

Vertigo is a sickening, whirling fear, a sensation of falling so acute, it actually made me fall—tipped my whole body sideways, away from the air side of the cliff into a precarious angle to solid ground. The Map flew out of my hand. My center of gravity lowered long enough for me to edge away from the abyss to a juniper tree, where I remained nearly prostrate so that the tree took the height and calmed my terrifying dizziness. As I regained my bearings, a pair of piñon jays burst out of the juniper, noisy with the hovering, high-pitched caw of a one-stroke crow. Nothing is more inseparable than this red desert and the sound of a piñon jay. Remove one from the other, and the air would fill with the terrible silence between toad song and the end of the world.

While I was busy retrieving equilibrium to the tilting protean sludge that was my head, the storm slipped off Navajo Mountain and engulfed the desert beyond the precipice. The sun disappeared, leaving a dim, greenish light and an eerie stillness. Panels of sheet lightning illuminated the clouds, then turned quickly to jagged ropes of fire, ratcheting up the violence. The juniper tree's pungent spice mixed with a shock-treatment blast of ozone. I had Reddi Kilowatt hair and a mouthful of metallic taste, as if the charged air had made my fillings into little batteries. When thunder changed from distant reverberations to an exploding minefield, it dawned on me that perhaps it was not a good idea to be fully exposed atop the highest point in a thirty-square-mile area in the belly of a monsoon, chumming in hundreds of volts of raw electricity with a handy unit of lightning bait: the oar pins on the raft frame.

Things suddenly grew more unruly. The temperature plummeted and the wind came up. Although it was not, the truck appeared to be uphill on a craggy mound, raising steel arms to the gods, ready to be the latest sacrifice to the ongoing collapse of the industrial state. Something perverse in me wanted to watch the tires melt. Nevertheless, I rose up and prepared to drive off the mesa to safer ground. Midsprint, I remembered the Map.

It is said that memory resides in the sense of smell; one whiff of juniper smoke, say, and the most poignant recollections flood forth. Instead, hearing was the sense that gave me the courage to return to the vertiginous brink, where lay the Map of the Known Universe, its silly pages fluttering in the blue wind.

The piñon jays had returned. The sound of their cries was, like the desert itself, edged, wild, and so familiar, I could hardly bear them. In a single moment the birds pitched me into a chasm of deepest, aching sorrow, sorrow because what I knew broke my heart. Someday (maybe today, if I fell off the cliff or lightning struck me) I would leave it all; all those glorious ways to feel the world—the hearing, smelling, seeing, touching, loving, wondering—would end in nothing. In the midst of this maelstrom I was certain that alive, too, I would be forever lost in this desert's deep, selfless beauty, literally killed by a magnificent obsession.

I am never able to tell the difference between luminosity and lunacy, so I cannot say which of the two sent me crawling on my hands and knees to the Map. Thunder crashed. Lightning sizzled, spun the finest of webs nearly within reach of my own hands. I tried to think of death not as nothingness but as a *change in the manner of existence.* I tried to think of Hopi jokes. I vowed to revive the Saint Thomas Aquinas Cactus and Succulent Society. Vertigo washed through me in nauseating waves. I was a lowly puddle of plasma, trading "I am alive" for a vague "I tend to exist" and weeping for joy over the sheer revelation. Then the Map's black scribblings, its tiny, pathetic hieroglyphics, grounded me.

In the sketchbook the Known Universe lay broken into pages. I had to suture the folios into a whole. As one piece, the Map became an overlay, a membrane. Residing on the Map meant not tending the territory. A map on paper turned my gaze away from the desert itself. I must raise my eyes.

It all fit beneath the belly of a lizard. River-polished stones, broken cliffs, skirts of talus clad in ricegrass and claret cup. Red dune fields marching to Colorado, weeds invading from Arizona. A river of inestimable grace, devout in its persistence to reach the sea. Sinuous red-rock canyons, sweet emerald jewels of springs, arroyos flowing with nothing. A sawed rib of uplifted sandstone, mountains packed together on the horizon like islands of prayer. Clay pots and wrist shells and the jumbled bones of wild geese and tender infants. The unimagined nearness of Pleistocene rain, lifting itself from subterranean bedrock to our lips. Tales of unimpeachable blessings, the path of a single life made visible. A coyote-trodden lowland with anxious rabbits and a small ditch that would soon overflow with the rain from this storm and, for the first time in recent memory, with the lusty song of hundreds of toads emerged from the dry desert dust, cued by the transient fury of a monsoon. There was but a single way to exist here, to make my way through this land with grace: take it into myself and rediscover it on my own breath.

A map does not disrupt sensuous connections with place; it merely abstracts them. Everything I needed was there in the Known Universe even as I never seemed to know what I was looking for. The desert spread below me as I clutched the small book to my chest. The rich, far-lost beauty of my home curved my breath. It required an attentiveness that was exhilarating and exhausting. Its colors and shapes pulled me right down below the skin of the world as I knew it.

Epilogue

The lives of desert toads alternate between suspended animation and animated frenzy. The strategy of dormancy and the explosive activity and hurried metamorphoses that follow it mirror the ephemeral conditions of the land itself. One moment the creatures lie beneath the ground, stalwart citizens of drought, shrink-wrapped in a membrane that keeps them alive—their own skin. The next moment they emerge to a world of water, song, wild sex, and predators.

Much time can pass between dormancy and activity. When the toads emerged on our bottomland during the summer monsoons, they sang all night for four nights straight. A few lovestruck young bufos wandered up to the new house and popcorned around my bare feet in the moonlight. I could find no one in town who recalled the last time the colony had been active. Instead, everyone commented on the heavier than usual rainstorms of the season, and more than one person reminded me that until we built our house on the bench above the river, there was no one but the cows and coyotes to hear the toads.

Before dawn on July 16, fifty years to the day of the world's first atomic bomb, I stood on ground zero again. The White Sands Missile Range had opened Trinity for the half-century anniversary. I came with a friend who guided a group from the Smithsonian Institution. Our group arrived in advance of a crowd that remained gridlocked in a long line of cars along the entry road. The stream of headlights snaked across the night desert, nearly five miles long.

Media crews, military personnel, and others—I do not know where they came from—clustered around the black obelisk that marked the monument. I stood in the dark at a distance, alone and near the fence that marked ground zero's perimeter. I held my eyes to the sky, my ears to the rain puddles, my nose to the wet creosote bushes. No one but nature was reenacting the event of a half century before. Just as it had on the night of Trinity, a summer monsoon soaked the Jornada del Muerto. A thin cloud cover remained, with no stars visible except through ragged patches over the Oscura Mountains.

At 5:29 A.M., the precise moment of record, someone stood beside me in the dark. But my attention was on the Oscuras, then on the monument itself, where in the harsh white light of the television cameras, a man threw blood on the obelisk and was wrestled to the ground by military police. As the daylight strengthened I noticed a scorched area outside the monument fence—charred creosote and soaptree yucca, prickly pear cactus with shriveled, blackened pads, a mask of black where the grasses once covered the ground. We must be vigilant of our warrior neighbors, I thought in bulbous understatement, lest they lose their grip on their own inventions and burn down the Universe again.

In the crowd of visitors everyone's eyes were riveted to the ground, searching for trinitite. I remembered the souvenirs in the gift shop of the atomic museum, the little chocolates shaped like Fat Man and Little Boy. Shouldn't we be looking at ourselves? I asked myself. Shouldn't we be looking straight into each other's eyes? I turned to the person next to me.

Earlier I had seen him leading a foreign camera crew. He was in his late fifties. He stood very quietly, hands behind his back, posture ramrod straight but not rigid. Without expression he watched the cenotaph. He was Japanese. It is possible to feel at once hollow and aflame, like a ghost burning. To have tears but crack with desiccation. To barely have enough muscles to lift one's own jawbone. When the fellow turned to me, it took all of my strength to lift and point with my chin to the nighthawks in the sky above us, cutting the pale dawn air in great swooping arcs.

Atoms are matter, but they also consist of a great deal of empty space, which anxious seekers of some*thing* might view as a lack of imagination on the part of nature. Electrons lie notably distant from their nucleus, separated by a void. As they peer deeper into the subatomic universe, scientists are discovering that as the scale of matter grows smaller, the emptiness between particles grows vaster. Physicists who study the smallest of particles call the spaces between them a *desert*. On his charts one physicist illustrates this emptiness with drawings of little saguaro cacti. Daily I aim myself at the palpable rapture of a cactus field. Home must be in there somewhere—I am still trying to find it. Home is both the mass and the space, the red-boned rock and the places where one tries to shape belief around mystery.

I am still looking for an aoudad and other weeds, the strange, exotic creatures that arrive in the Known Universe and take hold. I try to make visible to others those creatures that the desert grew itself, the inhabitants of those "empty" niches who truly may not be there if and when the fog of human hubris lifts. I still wonder if geography is fate, and what if the Known Universe had produced spices and orchids instead of uranium and a paradoxical zero point, where an act of creation can mean the complete absence of life. I fret less about a malaise of soul, rely more on simple motion and instinct as ways to tend the territory, and I end up carrying the sun-drenched land on my face, as most Colorado Plateau women do. I look into my coffee cup before I pour, and I try to live here as if there is no other place and it must last forever. It is the best we can do. Everyone's home is the heartland of consequence.

I often visit Tsé Valley, which is, after all, part of the neighborhood. On one trip I took the chunk of highway asphalt and taped to it my note from the Black Hole in Los Alamos: "Big cat. The Racal-Vadic VA3434." I still did not know what the hell a Racal-Vadic was. Let the archaeologists of the future figure it out. I jammed the asphalt chunk under the rubble near an old mine shaft. I put up a sign that said: NO DIGGING ALLOWED. THIS PLACE SHALL REMAIN BEAUTIFUL FOR 200,000 YEARS.

After burying the "yellow cake," I rested on a curve of slickrock with claret cup cactus and all of Tsé around me. In *The Names: A Memoir*, N. Scott Momaday wrote of this piece of Colorado Plateau:

The valley is vast. When you look out over it, it does not occur to you that there is an end to it. You see the monoliths that stand away in space, and you imagine that you have come upon eternity. They do not appear to exist in time. You think: I see that time comes to an end on this side of the rock, and on the other side there is nothing forever.

Across from me a voluptuous dune slid down the rim of a sandstone escarpment. Ricegrass, primrose, joint-fir, and other greenery sprouted from the coral sand. I heard sheep bells, and soon the flock itself made its way down the dune. A Navajo herder followed, singing a prayer. Momaday, too, wrote of two riders in this valley. "They were so far away that I could only barely see them, and their small, clear voices lay very lightly and for a long time on the distance between us."

Acknowledgments

I am indebted to many sources but wish to acknowledge these in particular: *The Making of the Atomic Bomb* by Richard Rhodes, *The Day the Sun Rose Twice* by Ferenc Szasz, and the archives of the Los Alamos National Laboratory. I owe thanks to poet-archaeologist Jonathan Till, to Cynthia Hermes for refuge in Santa Fe, and to Ellen Bradbury, who had her first security pass in Los Alamos at age six. For their guidance and support, I am grateful to Flip Brophy, William Strachan, and the Whiting Foundation. David Sobel gave fine shape to the wildest ideas.

In this book a few of the names of geographic places close to home have been changed.

Mark holds me together when I tend to fall apart. He built a magnificent house and took care of our wild places while I stayed behind to struggle. I am ready again: take me down the river.